I LOVE A PARADE

JUICY MOTHER

Number One: Celebration

Edited by Jennifer Camper

Soft Skull Press

Juicy Mother

First Edition

ISBN: 1-932360-70-0

Distributed by Publisher's Group West

1.800.788.3123 www.pgw.com

Printed in Canada

Book Design: Jennifer Camper

Soft Skull Press

71 Bond Street

Brooklyn, NY 11217

www.softskull.com

contents

introduction

Words and pictures together are damn powerful. Whether you call them sequential art, cartoons, comics or comix, drawings combined with text create some amazing art.

In the United States, comics for grown-ups are published as "alternative comix" and as graphic novels. The medium is slowly gaining more respect as an art form. Granted, the U.S. trails Asia, Europe and South America in this regard, and the economic prospects for most cartoonists are dismal. But, over time, there's been some small growth in opportunities for the creation of this kind of art – non-superhero, not-for-children, experimental, independent and ground-breaking comix.

And yet, something is missing. We all like to read comix relating to our own experiences of the world. Where are the comix for me, a Lebanese-American dyke? Back in the day there were titles like *Gay Comix, Wimmin's Comix, Real Girl* and *Tits and Clits*, but they're no longer published. Where are the comix by and about women, people of color and queers? I want an alternative to the alternative, but there are few venues for these stories.

And so *Juicy Mother* was born. Here is a home for the stories about the rest of us. Here are comix for Discerning Homosexuals, Uppity Ladies, Fierce People of Color and all their friends.

The theme for this issue is Celebration. Included are stories about an older butch dyke and her Lolita, an African-American gay man coming of age, an Arab Muslim dyke searching for her identity, two big hairy men getting married, and a cynical Latina teen battling the cosmos. Here, too is a cartoon jam – created when one artist draws a panel and passes it on to the next artist, who draws a panel and passes it on to the next artist, and so on, resulting in a glorious out-of-control comic.

Thanks and big wet kisses to all the contributors who created such brilliant art and patiently waited for *Juicy Mother* to become a reality.

Enjoy!

Jennifer Camper

MUST BE LOVE
©1995 DiMASSA
...AN' THEN SHE RAISED HER PINKIE UP LIKE THIS AND TAPPED HER FOOT! YA SHUDDA SEEN IT! SHE'S SO UNBELIEVABLE...
..AN SHE CAME OVER AFTER WORK LASSNITE AN' IT WAS SO HOT GASP AN' SHE DID THIS AN' SHE DID THAT..
SHE SHE SHE SO CUTE AN' THEN SHE AN' HER HER HER
HAW HAW! BOY, DID HE FUCK WITH THE WRONG PERSON!
PHEWF! WHAT'S HAPPENIN?
HORSE BEAT THE SHIT OUTTA SOME DICK WHO WAS HARASSING YVONNE!
HAW HAW!
WHAT HAPPENED?
HE WAS IN HER FACE GOIN' "WHAT ARE YA GONNA DO ABOUT IT, DYKE?
SO SHE JUMPS UP AND KICKS HIM LIKE TEN TIMES BEFORE HE EVEN KNOWS WHAT HIT 'IM!
HAW HAW HAW
HAH HA HA HA

...AND THEN THE COPS CAME AN' ARRESTED HIM!
AH HA HA HA HA HA HA HA HA HA HA
IS HORSE ALL RIGHT?
HUH! HER AND YVONNE BEEN DOIN' IT EVER SINCE! "MY HERO, MY HERO"
SLAM
JEEZIZ!
WHO THE F...
IT'S CRANK
DAMN!
SHE DON'T LOOK TOO HAPPY...
YEAH, WELL. SHE'S THE ONE WHO INSISTED ON NON-MONOGAMY!
MMM
SNORT
WHOOPS! ANOTHER "LIBERATED" COUPLE CRASHES INTO THE REALITY WALL!
SHIIIT! NON-MONOGAMY IS FOR DRUNKS AND PEOPLE WHO DON'T WANNA GET SERIOUS. IT AIN'T FOR FOLKS IN LOVE, NO WAY!
I'VE NEVER SEEN IT WORK FOR VERY LONG!
DON'T WALK AWAY FROM ME WHEN I'M IN MID-SENTENCE!
CRANK!
OOO, SHIT! HERE COMES DAISY!
ANYONE NOTICED ALL THE BREAK-UPS LATELY?
YEAH! IT'S LIKE SOME "DO OR DIE" SHIT IN THE AIR!
IT'S BECAUSE IT'S THE END OF THE MILLENIUM!!
HAWHAW!

LISTEN TO MS. 20 YEARS OLD! IT'S BEEN THE END OF THE MILLENIUM YOUR WHOLE LIFE!
SHUT UP WITH THAT AGE BULLSHIT!
Coffee NOW
DO IT HERE FREAKS -N- Queers!
OPEN EXCEPT WHEN WE'RE CLOSED
2000
YOU GONNA TELL ME THINGS DON'T FEEL A LITTLE WEIRDER THAN USUAL?
I DON'T KNOW WHAT "USUAL" IS ANYMORE!
SEE?
IT'S TRUE, EVERYTHING'S OUTTA CONTROL!
"OUTTA CONTROL!" WHAT COULD POSSIBLY BE OUTTA CONTROL? CERTAINLY NOT MY LIFE! HOW IS IT THAT TIME AFTER FUCKIN' TIME...
...I END UP IN A RELATIONSHIP WITH MY FUCKIN' FATHER?!?
HEY DAISY MAN WHAT'S HAPPENINNN YOU LOOK LIKE SOOO TWEAKED OH WOOOWWWW
I LOOK TWEAKED!?
HEY MANNN, DON'T LECTURE ME...
FUCK YOU, GWEN!
YA KNOW WHAT? I CAN'T DEAL WITH YOU ANYMORE! IT'S TOO DEPRESSING!

IT'S THE END-A THE WORLD, MAN! WHO GIVES A SHIT!!
ROBIN PROB'LY GIVES A SHIT!
DOES SHE KNOW YOU'RE OUT HERE ALL FUCKED UP AGAIN!?!
'AY MAN, MINE YER OWN BIZNISSS...
I WAS!
YOU'VE GOTTA BE KIDDING!
DID YOU JUST SAY THAT YOU LIKE THAT NOSE RING?
WELL...YEAH. IT LOOKS GOOD... ON HER...
IT LOOKS RIDICULOUS, AND I DON'T LIKE IT! SHE LOOKS LIKE A BULL!
CAFE CANDIDA
SNORT! WOULD'NT YOUR STUDENTS JUST LOVE IT IF YOU SHOWED UP WITH A NOSERING! HYORK!! HAH! WHAT NEXT? SHALL WE VISIT A TATTOO SHOP? HYAKK!!

GEEZ, ROBIN, I'M REALLY SORRY!
WELL, DON'T BE! IT'S A TOTAL RELIEF!
INDUSTRIAL APPLE JUICE
I SHOULDA KICKED HER OUT MONTHS AGO! HERE I AM TRYIN' TO STAY CLEAN..
..WITH HER USING RIGHT UNDER MY NOSE EVERY DAMN DAY!
GWEN'S A BIG GIRL... IF THAT'S WHAT SHE WANTS TO BE DOING THEN LET HER!
IT'S NOT MY PROBLEM ANYMORE!
MENU
ENOUGH ABOUT THAT! HOW ARE YOU?
OH, YOU KNOW.. GETTIN' USED TO GETTIN' DUMPED!
OH, RAY!
MENU
YEAH, WELL, KINDA GOES WITH THE TERRITORY SOMETIMES, YA KNOW? IT'LL EVEN OUT..
HEY, RAY?
HMM?
YOU KNOW WHAT? I'VE HAD A CRUSH ON YOU... FOR A REALLY LONG TIME... AND, UM, I THINK YOU SHOULD COME FOR DINNER... AT MY HOUSE... LIKE, TONIGHT.

OOPS! SCUSE ME! PARDON ME! OOPS! SORRY!
BOOF!
OH, HI HORSE!
HEY, RAY
WHAT'S UP?
OH, JUST GETTIN' SOME CHOW TO GO...
HOW'S YVONNE?
HEH HEH
GODDAMN GWEN! SHE LOOKS LIKE DEATH...
SHUDDER... THAT COULD TOTALLY HAPPEN... SOMEONE COULD WALK UP TO ME RIGHT NOW AND TELL ME GWEN O.D.'d AND SHE'S DEAD
AN' HERE I AM MAD AT HER... 'CAUSE SHE CAN'T FACE THE STINKING WORLD...
AND I'M MAD AT CRANK, TOO... TSK!
WE COULD ALL BE DEAD SOON... WE'RE LIVING IN A GODDAMN POLICE STATE PRACTICALLY
CLOSED
GET OUT
DIKES
2000
#8246-790
THIS GAY ESTABLIS
CLOSED
PER ORDER
U.S. GOVERNME
DIE QUEERS

MAYBE GWEN'S RIGHT! MAYBE IT IS THE END OF THE WORLD!!
TAN
I FELT A GODDAMN 'NOTHER EARTHQUAKE LAST NIGHT...
SHIT!
HELLO?
CRANK!? COME DOWN HERE!
BZZZ BZZZ
HELLO?
HEY, CLOVER!
HI, PAM! HOW ARE YA?
GOOD! HEY, I'M GONNA GO SEE THAT MOVIE, WANNA GO?
OOH, I CAN'T! I HAVE A DATE!
RIGHT ON! WITH P.J.?
YES!
WOW! THIS IS THE FOURTH ONE, NO?

YESSS!
CONGRATULATIONS! ISN'T THIS SORTA THE FIRST TIME SINCE...
YEAH...
AIRPORT SHUTTLE
...SINCE CHRIS DIED. I HAVEN'T DARED LET MYSELF FEEL ANYTHING FOR SO LONG... BUT I THINK I'M READY TO...
GOOD FOR YOU, CLOVER! GO FOR IT!
I AM GONNA GO FOR IT! YOU KNOW... I'M STILL AFRAID, BUT ONE THING I'VE LEARNED IS TO NEVER TAKE ANYTHING FOR GRANTED!!
RIGHT ON!
YEH, LIFE'S TOO...
GASP! OH, SHE'S HERE! GOTTA GO!!
OK! RIGHT ON! LATER!
BUZZZ
NOBODY...
WILL EVER REPLACE YOU, BABY...
SIGHHH~ HERE GOES...
hi
hi
FIN!

DOLLFACE
© 1999 BY STEPHEN WINTER & ROBERT KIRBY
TODAY IS MY BIRTHDAY. I'M OLD. FOR FAGS, THERE'S ONLY TWO AGES, YOUNG AND OLD, AND TODAY I AM DEFINITELY OLD.
AVENUE A
TEN YEARS AGO I WAS YOUNG. I WENT TO ART SCHOOL IN CHICAGO, DIDN'T SMOKE, DRINK, DO DRUGS, GET SEX OR HAVE ANY IDEA HOW THIN AND PRETTY I WAS.
MY "GAY ROLE MODEL" WAS A DAREDEVIL CUBAN SCULPTOR WHO COULD MONOLOGUE ENDLESSLY. HE THOUGHT I WAS FUN 'CAUSE I NEVER DISAGREED WITH HIM.
MENU
BREAKFAST SPECIALS
ONE NIGHT HE BUSTED IN TO DRAG ME TO SOME ACT-UP PARTY. APPARENTLY CHAPTERS FROM ACROSS THE COUNTRY WERE CONVERGING ON CHICAGO FOR A BIG DEMO. EVEN FOLKS FROM NEW YORK CITY!
"ACT-UP"?
THE SECOND I WALKED IN I REALIZED THIS WAS A HUGE MISTAKE. I WAS TOO TALL, TOO SKINNY, TOO YOUNG AND TOO UNPOLITICAL.
HA HA HA
HA
FIGHT THE POWERS THAT BE

BUT I ALWAYS FELT LIKE THAT. FINALLY, I SAW SOMEONE I KNEW. HE HAD ALREADY MET THIS HOT NUMBER FROM SEATTLE.
TRAV!
HEY DARLIN'! HOW YA DOIN'? I'D LIKE YOU TO MEET, UH... UM, DAN?
THEN I SAW.....
THE SMITHS
IT'S DAVE...
HE LOOKED LIKE THIS BOY I'D SEEN IN SOME DISNEY MOVIE YEARS AGO, RED HAIR AND A COTTON-CANDY SMILE....
I STARTED TO APPROACH BUT THEN I CAUGHT MYSELF IN THE MIRROR.
WHY WOULD HE EVER WANT ME..?
SHIT!
THE SMITHS
HE ALWAYS GOT ANY BOY HE WANTED!
SNIFF
SNIFF
SNIFF
SOMEONE ADJUSTED THE STEREO AND SUDDENLY EVERYONE WAS SLOW-DANCING....
HIV +
HEY...!
..WANNA DANCE?
!

SO HE WENT TO NYU IN NEW YORK(!!!), MAJORED IN DRAMA (DON'T THEY ALL?) AND WAS FLYING ON COCAINE.. BUT HE WAS SO TOTALLY INTO ME, HE LOOKED RIGHT AT ME LIKE HE SAW ME! HE LIKED ME! IN A WAY THAT NO ONE HAD BEFORE.....
THE
HOW CAN YOU MEND THIS BROKEN MAN
HOW CAN A LOSER EVER WIN
I WAS RELIEVED HE DIDN'T WANNA STAY WHEN THE ORGY BEGAN...
...FOR A BUNCH OF AIDS ACTIVISTS I NOTICED VERY FEW CONDOMS..
SPLOIT!
WE WENT BACK TO MY PLACE. THAT WAS MY FIRST NIGHT OF ANAL SEX. HE WAS FREAKING ME OUT A LITTLE 'CAUSE HE WAS ON SO MANY DRUGS BUT IT WAS GOOD.
OW!
WOW!
OOH YEAH BABY
I ALWAYS WONDERED IF MY PARENTS HEARD US...
AFTERWARDS, THIS HORRIBLE FEELING CAME OVER ME LIKE I'D BEEN HOLLOWED OUT WITH A SHOVEL.
HE HELD ME AND ROCKED ME.

I KNEW AT THAT MOMENT THAT HE LOVED ME AND I LOVED HIM AND WE'D BE TOGETHER FOREVER AND HE'D ASK ME TO MOVE TO NEW YORK WITH HIM AND I'D FINISH SCHOOL THERE AND WE'D LIVE TOGETHER IN THE GLAMOROUS GRUNGE OF THE EAST VILLAGE UNTIL HE WON HIS FIRST TONY AND I HAD A SOLO AT THE GUGGENHEIM. OH HOW WONDERFUL TO HAVE FOUND TRUE LOVE SO YOUNG
Z
BRAAP
FOR THE NEXT COUPLE OF DAYS I RARELY SLEPT, BARELY ATE, AND HAD TONS OF SEX. WE MARCHED.... CHANTED.... AND WERE HELD IN A HOLDING CELL FOR SIX HOURS! WE DECIDED TO START A KISS-IN, WHICH WAS APPARENTLY AGAINST THE LAW, SO WE WERE SEPARATED.
ACT UP SILENCE=DEATH
THE GOVERNMENT HAS BLOOD ON IT'S HANDS
SHAME SHAME
LET'S GO, FAGGOT
SEE YA
YEAH BYE
THEN SOME DYKES STARTED A TATTOO FASHION SHOW AND EVERYTHING GOT FUN AGAIN.
WOO WOO
CLAP CLAP
YOU GO GIRLS!
IT WAS LIKE I BELONGED.
WE WERE FINALLY RELEASED ON OUR OWN RECOGNIZANCE.
WHERE'D HE GO?
YOUR PLACE?

FOR SOME REASON HE DIDN'T SEEM AS HAPPY TO SEE ME AS BEFORE.
HEY!
10 MOST WANTED
OH, HI.
THE SEX WAS DIFFERENT NOW. HE DIDN'T SEEM TO BE ALL THERE. AFTERWARDS, WHEN I BEGAN TO FEEL HOLLOW AGAIN, HE JUST WENT TO SLEEP.
THE NEXT MORNING WAS SOME RADICAL FAERIE TREE LOVE CEREMONY OR SOMETHING. I THOUGHT IT WAS A BIT MUCH BUT I DIDN'T WANT THE WEEKEND TO BE OVER.
BE BACK IN A BIT!
C'MON!
OH, SUN BLOSSOM
THEY WERE PROBABLY GOING OFF TO DO DRUGS. IT WAS A RELIEF TO BE AWAY FROM HIM FOR A WHILE. I WONDERED VAGUELY IF HE WOULD GIVE ME HIS NUMBER IN NEW YORK.
THE ONLY OTHER BLACK PERSON THERE WAS THIS GUY I HAD ASKED OUT ONCE FOR COFFEE, BUT HE'D STOOD ME UP. I'D SEEN HIM LATER WITH SOME WHITE BOY BUT NEVER ASKED HIM WHY.
OOOH, HUN-AY!
TWO QUEENS CAME BACK FROM A THRIFT STORE AND STARTED PASSING AROUND THE FINERY. SOME OF IT WAS FABULOUS....
....AND SOME OF IT WAS NOT.
ISN'T SHE PRECIOUS?

THINGS LIKE THIS... THIS MEANS BAD THINGS FOR ME. I DON'T LIKE IT.
IT'S NOT CUTE.
I AGREE.
HEY, WHAT'S GOING ON?
OHHHHH, IT'S A LITTLE YOU-DOLL! NOW I'LL ALWAYS HAVE YOU WITH ME!
what?
BOND ST.
THE END

© July 2003 Ariel Schrag

what the...
oh
it's just wandering hands

wandering hands!
wandering hands!
heeheeheeh heeeheheee

hey, you can crash here if you want
thanks
wandering hands

© ALISON BECHDEL

what I know now about... being an *Oppressed Minority Cartoonist*

I WASN'T ALWAYS AN OPPRESSED MINORITY CARTOONIST. AS A CHILD, I DREW WHATEVER THE HELL I FELT LIKE.
CRANS
Mr. and Mrs. Bunny
BUT ONCE I REALIZED I WAS AN OPPRESSED MINORITY, THOSE DAYS WERE GONE. FROM THAT POINT ON, ALL I DREW WAS CARTOONS ABOUT MY OPPRESSED MINORITY GROUP.
I'M AN OP-PRESSED MI·NO·RI·TEE AND I'M OKAY!
I DRAW ALL NIGHT, AND I SLEEP ALL DAY!
ACTUALLY, FOR A LONG TIME THIS WAS NOT A PROBLEM.
IT DIDN'T BOTHER ME THAT MY CARTOONS WERE NOT IN THE NEW YORKER, OR THAT MY BOOKS WERE RELEGATED TO ONE OF THE "OPPRESSED MINORITY STUDIES" SHELVES.
IT'S NOT BECAUSE I SUCK, IT'S BECAUSE I'M AN OPPRESSED MINORITY.
HETERO-PATRIARCHAL SCUM.
AND I WAS NOT ONE OF THOSE SELF-LOATHING OPPRESSED MINORITIES WHO WAS ASHAMED OF BEING AN OPPRESSED MINORITY.
I'M A WRITER, AND I'M A MEMBER OF AN OPPRESSED MINORITY, BUT I'M NOT AN OPPRESSED MINORITY WRITER!
ASSIMILATIONIST SCUM! I WAS PROUD TO BE AN OPPRESSED MINORITY CARTOONIST!
IT'S TRUE, I HAD HOPES THAT ONE DAY MY COMIC STRIP WOULD BE READ NOT JUST BY MEMBERS OF MY OPPRESSED MINORITY GROUP, BUT BY REGULAR PEOPLE TOO.
HA!
WHAT'S GOING ON IN "OPPRESSED MINORITIES TO WATCH OUT FOR" TODAY, MOTHER?
PADUCAH PICAYUNE
COORS
I WOULD NOT KOWTOW TO THEIR BOURGEOIS TASTES, BUT WOULD MAINTAIN THE OPPRESSED MINORITY AUTHENTICITY OF MY CHARACTERS. THE MASSES WOULD LOVE ME ANYWAY.
ONE OF THE GALS ACCIDENTALLY RAN HER DILDO THROUGH THE FAX MACHINE.
YE-OWCH! WAS IT STRAPPED ON?

WHEN THIS DREAM FAILED TO MATERIALIZE, I GREW BITTER. IF ONLY I'D WAITED FOR A MORE OPPORTUNE TIME TO REVEAL MY OPPRESSED MINORITY STATUS.
YES, IT'S TRUE. I'M A BIG OLE OPPRESSED MINORITY. THANKS FOR WATCHING ALL THESE YEARS. NOW I'M GOING OFF THE AIR TO LIVE IN RETIRED SPLENDOR.
I LONG FOR THE FREEDOM OF MY CHILDHOOD. BUT AFTER ALL THESE YEARS OF DRAWING OPPRESSED MINORITIES, IT'S HARD TO GO BACK.
DAMN.
TIME HAS TAKEN ITS TOLL, AND BEING AN OPPRESSED MINORITY CARTOONIST IS NOT AS CHEAP AS IT USED TO BE.
SINGLE MALT SCOTCH
PRESCRIPTION MIGRAINE MEDICATION
WHY COULDN'T I JUST HAVE BEEN A CARTOONIST? WHY DID GOD HAVE TO MAKE ME AN OPPRESSED MINORITY CARTOONIST?!
RING!
LOCH NESS
ALL I CAN SAY IS, THANK GOD FOR AFFIRMATIVE ACTION.
YOU WANT ME TO DO A PIECE FOR THE SPECIAL OPPRESSED MINORITY PRIDE ISSUE OF "THE STRANGER"?
EVEN THOUGH YOU'D NEVER RUN MY COMIC STRIP IN THE REGULAR PAPER, YOU OPPRESSIVE ALTERNATIVE WEEKLY SCUM?!
WHY, IT WOULD BE AN HONOR!

a comic strip by Serena Pillai
THE ITALIAN COUSIN
dedicato a C.Z.
THE AIRPORT TERMINAL IS CROWDED WITH COMMUTERS, LIKE EVERY FRIDAY
EIGHT O' CLOCK... SHE SHOULD HAVE ALREADY ARRIVED ...
ARRIVALS
A PHOTO OF HER WHEN SHE WAS 10 NOW SHE'S 15, I DON'T KNOW IF I'LL BE ABLE TO SPOT HER...
SHIT... I HAVE TO BABYSIT A SILLY NAGGING 15-YEAR-OLD GIRL...
AND TONIGHT I COULD HAVE SEEN NOREEN... DOUBLE SHIT !!
ALITALIA AZ 0133 FROM ROME DUE AT 20.00 HAS A DELAY OF 20 MINUTES
LATE, AS ITALIANS ALWAYS ARE!
DEPARTURES
ARRIVALS
25 MINS. AND SEVERAL PINTS LATER
ALITALIA AZ 0133 FROM ROME LANDING NOW
AT LAST!
1

HEAVENS ABOVE!! THERE MUST BE HUNDREDS OF 15 YEAR OLDS!
MARIA!
GIUSEPPE!
CIAO, MARCO!
?
!
MARINA?...
CRISTIANA, I SUPPOSE!
JUST TYPICAL! YOU THINK YOU'LL MEET A KID AND YOU FIND A BLOOMING GIRL! WE ALWAYS FORGET HOW QUICKLY BABIES GROW UP, ESPECIALLY WHEN THEY HAPPEN TO BE OUR COUSINS...
OK, YOUNG MISS! I'VE GOT SOME PLANS READY FOR YOU! VCR, FREE HOCKEY TICKETS, MOVIES...
I'M AN ICE HOCKEY REFEREE, I COULD INTRODUCE YOU TO THE GAME, I'M SURE YOU'LL LIKE IT...
BESIDES, YOUR ENGLISH SCHOOL WILL TAKE CARE OF
EHM... MARINA, WHAT ARE YOU DOING?
I LIKE YOU, CHRIS! I ALWAYS LIKED YOU, AND I WANT TO MAKE LOVE WITH YOU!
2

MARINA... WHAT ARE YOU SAYING? YOU'RE A KID, I COULD BE YOUR DAD!
ARE YOU IMPLYING THAT TEENAGERS ARE NOT ENTITLED TO HAVE SEX OR WHAT...?
LISTEN, MARINA, I'M YOUR COUSIN, I'M 20 YEARS OLDER THAN YOU AND I'M MARRIED TO A WONDERFUL WOMAN!
BLEAH!
CHRIS, I WANT YOU AND YOU WANT ME! YOU DON'T KNOW IT YET BUT YOU WILL SOON! AND YOUR GIRLFRIEND IS JUST A WORN-OUT EXCUSE!
JUST WHAT I NEEDED! A 15-YEAR-OLD PAIN IN THE ASS YELLING AT ME. HOW LONG DO YOU FANCY STAYING IN THE STATES?
THAT EVENING I HAD TO UMPIRE A BIG MATCH: WOLVES~BEARS, VALID FOR THE MAJOR LEAGUE QUALIFICATION
YOU'LL ENJOY IT, GAL!
PFFF... MAY I BE EXEMPTED?
NO!
WOLVES~BEARS FOR THE LEAGUE
MAJORETTES! BLEAH!
GO GO BEARS!
WHAT ARE YOU READING?
"THE PRINCE"
WOW! I LIKE PRINCE, TOO!
BY NICCOLO' MACHIAVELLI!
WHO?
SUDDENLY, AFTER 1/4 HOUR OF THE MATCH...
WHEE WHEE WHE
WHAT IS IT?
I'M TURNING DEAF!
IT'S THE GENERAL ALARM!
...THE SAFETY SYSTEM WENT HAYWIRE AND MARINA...
WHEE WHEE WHEE WHEE WHE
PAPÉ SATÁN PAPÉ SATÁN I INVOKE THE POWER OF THE BEAST... 666 TIMES I INVOKE YOU BEELZEBUB
LISTEN TO THY PRIESTESS MAKE THIS BLOODY SIREN SHUT UP...
3

WHEE WHEE WHE
IN THIS UNHOLY PLACE FREE US OF THIS HORRIBLE SOUND; TAKE THIS INNOCENT CHILD AS AN OFFERING...
HEY, MY GRANDSON!
BUT... WHAT THE XXX IS SHE DOING?
AND AS SOON AS SHE FINISHED HER SPEECH...
WHE...!! CLICK!
THANK YOU, LORD OF THE FLIES!
COOL!
HEY YOU! KEEP YOUR HANDS OFF MY BOY!
SHE'S A SATANIST!
SHE'S A PRIESTESS OF THE ANTICHURCH!
SHE WAS READING MACHIAVELLI, AN OCCULTIST!
SHE'S ITALIAN!
SHE'S A SLUT
WOW! GRAN, AM I THE CHOSEN VICTIM?
SHHH... KISS THIS HOLY CROSS...
I CAN'T BELIEVE IT!
JESUS, I LAUGHED SO MUCH! BUT LATER, AFTER A NICE SHOWER AND A SANDWICH...
THIS IS NOREEN'S ANSWERING MACHINE. I'M NOT AT HOME, BUT...
CLICK
... CHRIS... MAY I... ?
I WAS JUST WONDERING IF THERE'S ANYTHING WE NEED, I'M GOING OUT!
?!! MARINA!!?
JESUS, WHATCHA MEAN GOING OUT DRESSED LIKE THAT?
I DIDN'T COME HERE TO SEE CARTOONS ON TV. AM I NOT FREE TO GO OUT IN THE LAND OF DEMOCRACY?
OF COURSE YOU COULD ESCORT ME LIKE A TRUE GENTLEMAN, CONSIDERED THAT SHE ISN'T AT HOME WAITING FOR YOU...
4

JESUS! WHAT DID I DO TO DESERVE SUCH A PEST? **HOW COULD I ACCEPT TO PUT A 15-YEAR-OLD UP?**
GRANNY'S MONEY! REMEMBER, CHRIS?
PLOP
CRISTIANA, CARA! NON VOGLIO CHE MARINA ALLOGGI DA ESTRANEI... VANNO BENE $ 2,000 PER IL TUO DISTURBO?
$ 2,000 TO PUT THE BABY UP FOR 3 WEEKS? **OK GRAN!** CERTO, NONNA!
SO, ARE YOU COMING WITH ME?
GRRR...
♥ OH CHRIS, YOU'RE WONDERFUL, I'M GOING TO OFFER YOU A GREAT DINNER... I LOVE YOU ♥
DON'T KISS ME IN THE EAR!
AFTER MUCH DISCUSSION ABOUT THE RESTAURANT WE DECIDED TO GO TO **THE PUNJAB PEARL**, ONE OF THE MOST EXCLUSIVE RESTAURANTS IN THE CITY. SHE LIKED TO WASTE HER MONEY ALL RIGHT...
...COFFEE, BRANDY, SIR?
HUM...
5

ANOTHER SPOONFUL OF GINGER SAUCE, CHRIS? IT'S AN APHRODISIAC GOOD FOR BUTCHES...
FOR GOD'S SAKE, STOP TEASING ME!
LISTEN MARINA, I'M GOING TO THE JOHN AND THEN RIGHT HOME! I'VE HAD ENOUGH OF YOUR WHIMS! AND THAT'S FINAL!
YOU DON'T BELIEVE ME, DO YOU CHRIS, BUT I TELL YOU WE WILL MAKE LOVE!
SHE'S AS STUBBORN AS A MULE...
I'LL NEVER UNDERSTAND BUTCHES...
TZK!
ZAK
I WANT HER! SHE'S THE ONE
WHY DOESN'T SHE WANT ME...
FSSSS
HELLO, MACHO MAN!
HI, DOLL!
I FEEL SO LONELY TONIGHT!
HOW MUCH ARE YOU?
MMH... I DON'T KNOW IF YOU CAN AFFORD THIS...
WHITE
1000
IT'S A FUCKING LOT OF MONEY! FOR $1,000 I WANT EVERYTHING
FULL OPTION
YOU'LL HAVE EVERYTHING!
OK BABY!

CHRIS, I THINK THAT MAN WANTS TO TALK TO YOU
EXCUSE ME, SIR, I WANTED TO HIRE YOUR GIRL FOR THE NIGHT IF I'M NOT WRONG, THE FEE IS $1,000...
OF COURSE FOR THIS SUM I RECKON I'LL SCRATCH HER FITTINGS HERE AND THERE, AND PERHAPS I'LL MAKE HER BLEED ...HOPE YOU DON'T MIND...
...NOT AT ALL... LET'S DEFINE OUR TRANSACTION AT THE PARKING LOT, SIR!
SO, YOU LIKE LITTLE GIRLS, DON'T YOU, YOU PIG!
I BEG YOUR PAR...
WHAT DID YOU SAY ABOUT SCRATCHING HER?
NO, NOT THERE!
AND ABOUT BLEEDING?
SOCK!
THUD
UGH!
SHE'S ONLY 15, YOU BASTARD! 15!
CHRIS... ARE YOU HURT?
RIGHT HOME! AND SHUDUP!
THE DAY AFTER, MARINA'S 2nd DAY IN AMERICA...
NOW, YOUNG LADY, YOU GET YOUR ASS RIGHT OFF TO SCHOOL AND STAY THERE UNTIL EVENING, GOT IT?
IT'S SATURDAY, CHRIS SCHOOL WILL ONLY START ON MONDAY...
WHAT? THE WHOLE WEEK-END WITH YOU AROUND... I'M RINGING GRAN AND I'LL WITHDRAW...
RIIING!
YES... WHO IS IT? OH... IT'S FOR YOU
THANKS!
7

ALLORA, COCCA, HAI SCOPATO BENE STANOTTE?
AH-AH-AH! E TU HAI CAGATO BENE, CHÈ DI SCOPARE NON SE NE PARLA?
U-UH! LA NOSTRA MARINA È ANCORA VERGINE!
MAI STATA! SONO ARIETE, IO!
BEH, TELEFONAMI QUANDO AVRAI PARTICOLARI INTERESSANTI DA RACCONTARE!
NON TI DIRÓ NULLA PER NON FARTI SCOPPIARE D' INVIDIA!
CIAO MARI!
CIAO BELLA!
HELLO DUCK! SCREWED OR STILL A VIRGIN? A-AH! AND YOU, CRAPPED OR STILL FULL OF IT?
MMH... VIRGIN... PHONE ME BACK WHEN YOU'VE GOT INTERESTING DETAILS...
AAAURGH
I DON'T WANNA GET ANOTHER CALL IN THE WORLD, I'M GONNA BURY MYSELF IN MY ROOM UNTIL MONDAY IS IT FINE, LIKE THIS?
FINE!
2 HOURS LATER...
JOHN SPEAKS ENGLISH
WE DON'T SPEAK RUSSIAN
THEY SPEAK GERMAN
MARINA, MAY I?
KNOCK
KNOCK
IT'S YOUR HOUSE!
PERFECT ENGLISH
MARINA, FANCY COMING TO THE ZOO WITH ME?
THE ZOO? JESUS...
CHRIS, IS IT SO HARD FOR YOU TO REALIZE THAT I'M NO LONGER A KID? AND WHAT ON EARTH MADE YOU THINK I WOULD LIKE TO SEE A PRISON FOR ANIMALS?
JANE DOESN'T SPEAK ITALIAN
I'M JUST TRYING TO MANAGE! I NEVER FACED THIS STUFF BEFORE. I'M NOT USED TO 15-YEAR-OLD PEOPLE!
16 NEXT MONTH
O.K., 16. I'M TRYING TO DO MY BEST.
REALLY
I APPRECIATE IT!
DON'T CRY MARINA I LOVE YOU!
REALLY?
YES
SO, DO YOU WANT TO STAY HERE OR GO OUT WITH ME?
OH CHRIS!
O.K. GET DRESSED YOUNG LADY, WE'RE HAVING LUNCH WITH NOREEN!
NOREEN?!
8

NOREEN IS A PERFECT FEMME. SHE JUST KNOWS HOW TO CUDDLE HER BUTCH. SHE'S A BIT OF A DRAG, THOUGH...
♫ OH, CHRIS, DO YOU REALLY NEED THAT EXTRA HELPING OF ROAST BEEF ?♫
CRUNCH
CHEW
YUP!
SO, YOU'RE CHRIS'S ITALIAN COUSIN. HOW OLD ARE YOU, DEAR ?
OLD ENOUGH!
OH OH OH! ITALIAN HUMOUR! DELICIOUS! AND WHAT DO YOU DO IN ITALY?
I HAVE FUN!
MMHH... SPORTS? HOBBIES?
SEX! KINKY SEX!
OH LA LA! ISN'T IT A BIT EARLY FOR THAT?
ONLY FOR PRUDES!
EHEM... THERE'S A MATCH ON T.V. WANNA SEE IT?
PARDON?
AND THERE'S THE QUIZ SHOW ON A.B.C....
YOU'RE A HYPOCRITICAL PURITAN!
MMHHH... CHRIIIS! AREN'T YOU FORGETTING THAT MEETING AT THE CLUB AT 5.00!
UH-UUH! WHAT AN EXCITING PROGRAM!
MARINA! SHUT UP! YOU'RE BEING REALLY RUDE!
NEVER MIND, CHRIS! I'LL WAIT FOR YOU AT 4.30, UNDER 18S ARE NOT INVITED!
DON'T WORRY MUMMY I JUST HOPE I WON'T BE LIKE YOU AT 50!
I'M 40!
WELL, YOU LOOK 50!
UMPFT...
YOU SAID THOSE MEETINGS ARE A LETHAL BORE!
YUP, BUT NOREEN IS TOO INTO THEM FOR ME TO IGNORE THEM!
YOUR NOREEN IS A BORE, TOO!
NOPE, SHE'S FUN!
SHE WAS, YOU MEAN? I BET SHE'S ROUTINE JUST LIKE LUNCH AT 2.00 OR BED AT 11.30! AM I WRONG?
CUT IT MARINA!
BUT YOU DON'T CARE A DAMN ABOUT THE BLOODY MEETING!
MY WIFE ORGANIZED IT!
WHO ARE YOU KIDDING? ME?
NO, MARINA! PERHAPS JUST MYSELF!
9

LATER, AT HOME...
ANYWAY, I HAVE TO SHAVE!
OH, CHRIS, MAY I SHAVE YOU?
I CAN SHAVE, YOU KNOW! I LEARNED WHEN I WAS 12!
THIS IS MY RAZOR. I SOMETIMES USE IT TO SHAVE DAD. I LIKE IT!
C'MON, CHRIS! LET ME TRY!
O.K. MARINA, BUT IF YOU HURT ME YOU WILL GO TO A HOTEL WITH NO COMPLAINING (NOR TELLING GRAN, OF COURSE)
OH, CHRIS, YOU WON'T REGRET IT!
♥SMACK♥ I LOVE YOU CHRIS!
OH JESUS! SHE'S SOOO SWEET...
O.K. SHAVE ME!
YOU WON'T MOVE, WILL YOU?
YOU MUST STAY PERFECTLY STILL AND RELAXED!
A-AH!
DON'T MOVE... DON'T TALK AND SHUT YOUR EYES
M-MMH!

SHUT THEM! IF YOU DON'T TRUST ME I WON'T SHAVE YOU!
O.K. FEEL RELAXED? FREE YOUR MIND AND ENJOY THE SHAVING...
DO YOU LIKE THIS SINGER? HER NAME'S CARMEN CONSOLI
ZZZIIIKKKHHHH!
DON'T MOVE
ZZZIIIIK!
...MMH... YOUR SHAVING FOAM SMELLS SO GOOOD...
ZZZIIIKKK!
WELL, IT WAS CHEAP ENOUGH..
SSSHH...
DON'T MOVE G'DAY HANDSOME!
ZZIIIK
BUT! WHAT...
FINISHED, OOH
MARINA! WHAT THE HELL ARE YOU DOING?
SITTING ON YOUR HAND, CHRIS!
I WANT YOU, CHRIS! GOD! WHAT MUST I DO TO MAKE LOVE WITH YOU? FEEL HOW WET I AM!
MARINA... I CAN'T DO IT ... I JUST CAN'T... ... PLEASE...
YES, YOU CAN, HONEY YOU CAN!
JESUS CHRIST... WHAT AM I DOING?
OH CHRIS, CHRIS...
PLEASE DON'T HURT ME... IT'S THE FIRST TIME ...
I KNOW SUGAR YOU SMELL LIKE A VIRGIN... TRUST ME, AS I TRUSTED YOUR RAZOR!
THAT AFTERNOON WAS WONDERFUL, MARINA WAS ALL THRILLS AND MOANS UNDER ME, A PRECIOUS MUSICAL INSTRUMENT SINGING HER DEBUT
...HER EYES OPEN WIDE IN BEWILDERMENT AT THE SWEETNESS AND POWER OF PASSION, GROWING INSIDE HER UNTIL THE ORGASMIC EXPLOSION...
RING RING

CHRIS, NOREEN HERE... CHRIS? ARE YOU JOINING US AT THE CLUB OR NOT? IT'S THE THIRD MESSAGE I'VE LEFT IN THE BLOODY MACHINE...
I'M WAITING FOR YOU, HONEY...
ARE YOU GOING?
ZERO!
NO MEETING IN THE WORLD IS INTERESTING ENOUGH TO STOP SUCH BEAUTIFUL LOVEMAKING
OH CHRIS...
CHRIS... LET ME DO TO YOU WHAT YOU'VE JUST DONE TO ME
MMHHH SLOWLIER SUGAR... I DON'T WANT TO COME TOO EARLY...
SHE MADE GREAT LOVE TO ME, SWEET AND STRONG, THE BEST LOVE I'D HAD FOR MONTHS. I STILL QUAVER AT THE THOUGHT OF IT.
AAH.. AAAAHH..AH..AH..
1 HOUR LATER
CHRIS, I DON'T WANT TO UPSET YOUR RELATIONSHIP WITH NOREEN...
NEVER MIND LOVE! THINGS WILL SETTLE DOWN IN A DAY OR 2!
WILL YOU TELL HER?
NOPE. I DON'T THINK IT'S A GOOD IDEA!
WE JUST HAD AN ARGUMENT ABOUT POLY-MONO RELATIONSHIP, AND BELIEVE ME, I DON'T WANNA GO INTO IT AGAIN! UGH!
12

WHERE ARE YOU TAKING ME, LOVE?
SIGHTSEEING...
AND YOU, SUGAR, WILL YOU TELL YOUR FRIENDS?
OF COURSE NOT. IT'S MY PRIVATE LIFE! ... GOING TO THE LADIES'...
...UNA SCOPATA COSMICA! STASERA TI MANDO I DETTAGLI VIA INTERNET!
A COSMIC SCREW! I'LL TELL YOU THE DETAILS VIA INTERNET TONIGHT
DAVVERO? BEAATAAAA!
CIN CIN MARI
REALLY!?! LUCKY YOU!
WHAT A LITTLE WHORE!
FSSS
CHRIS... COULD YOU TAKE ME TO THE FUNFAIR NOW?
FUNFAIR? I THOUGHT YOU WERE TOO OLD FOR THESE THINGS!
OH PLEEEASE, CHRIS! DON'T MOCK ME! BE A GENTLEMAN!
O.K. YOUNG LADY! HEY! DON'T KISS ME IN THE EAR!
THE END
13

Auntie Moo's Typewriters

by Howard Cruse

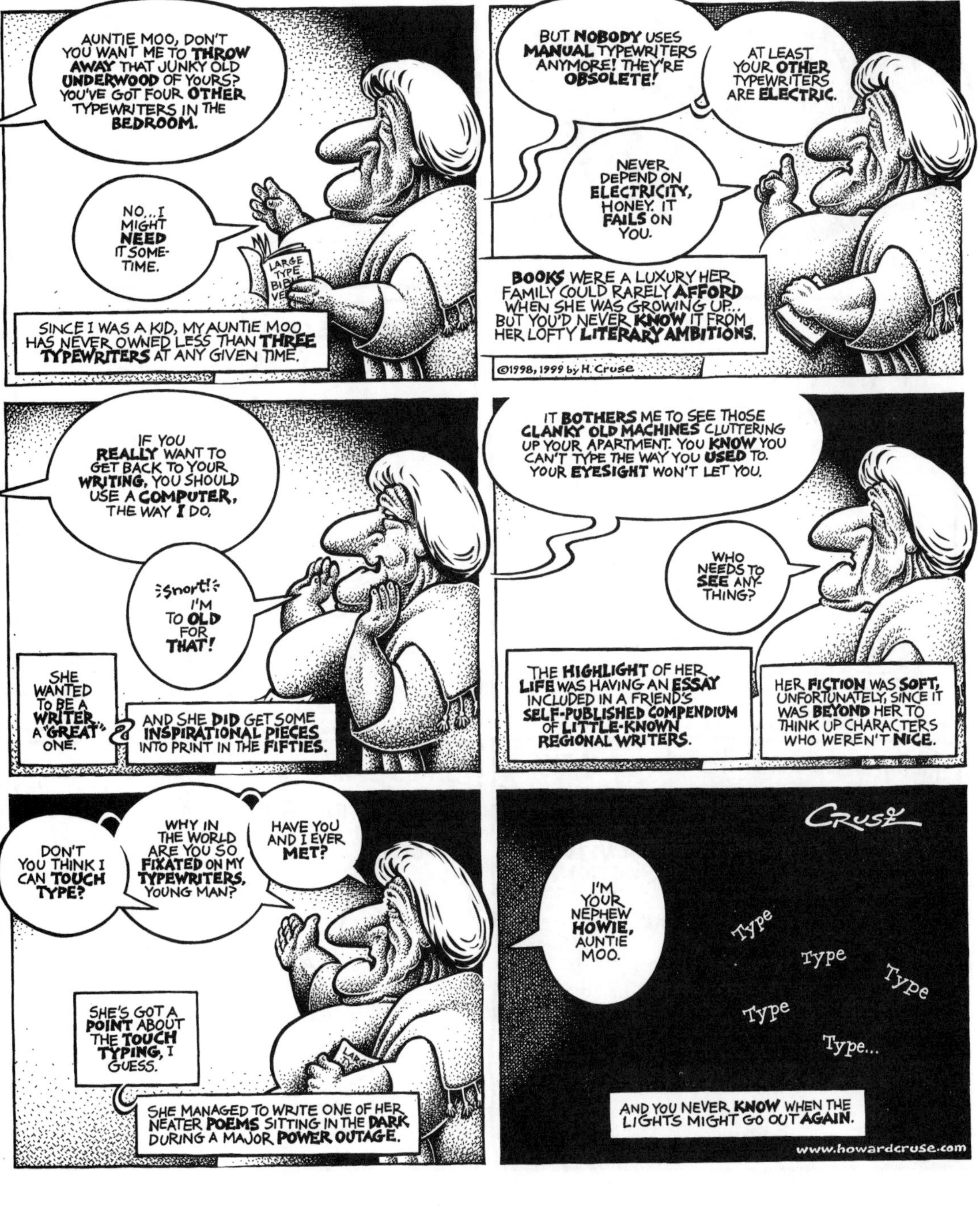

AUNTIE MOO, DON'T YOU WANT ME TO THROW AWAY THAT JUNKY OLD UNDERWOOD OF YOURS? YOU'VE GOT FOUR OTHER TYPEWRITERS IN THE BEDROOM.
NO... I MIGHT NEED IT SOMETIME.
LARGE TYPE BIB
SINCE I WAS A KID, MY AUNTIE MOO HAS NEVER OWNED LESS THAN THREE TYPEWRITERS AT ANY GIVEN TIME.
BUT NOBODY USES MANUAL TYPEWRITERS ANYMORE! THEY'RE OBSOLETE!
AT LEAST YOUR OTHER TYPEWRITERS ARE ELECTRIC.
NEVER DEPEND ON ELECTRICITY, HONEY. IT FAILS ON YOU.
BOOKS WERE A LUXURY HER FAMILY COULD RARELY AFFORD WHEN SHE WAS GROWING UP... BUT YOU'D NEVER KNOW IT FROM HER LOFTY LITERARY AMBITIONS.
©1998, 1999 by H. Cruse
IF YOU REALLY WANT TO GET BACK TO YOUR WRITING, YOU SHOULD USE A COMPUTER, THE WAY I DO.
Snort! I'M TO OLD FOR THAT!
SHE WANTED TO BE A WRITER. A "GREAT" ONE.
AND SHE DID GET SOME INSPIRATIONAL PIECES INTO PRINT IN THE FIFTIES.
IT BOTHERS ME TO SEE THOSE CLANKY OLD MACHINES CLUTTERING UP YOUR APARTMENT. YOU KNOW YOU CAN'T TYPE THE WAY YOU USED TO. YOUR EYESIGHT WON'T LET YOU.
WHO NEEDS TO SEE ANYTHING?
THE HIGHLIGHT OF HER LIFE WAS HAVING AN ESSAY INCLUDED IN A FRIEND'S SELF-PUBLISHED COMPENDIUM OF LITTLE-KNOWN REGIONAL WRITERS.
HER FICTION WAS SOFT, UNFORTUNATELY, SINCE IT WAS BEYOND HER TO THINK UP CHARACTERS WHO WEREN'T NICE.
DON'T YOU THINK I CAN TOUCH TYPE?
WHY IN THE WORLD ARE YOU SO FIXATED ON MY TYPEWRITERS, YOUNG MAN?
HAVE YOU AND I EVER MET?
SHE'S GOT A POINT ABOUT THE TOUCH TYPING, I GUESS.
SHE MANAGED TO WRITE ONE OF HER NEATER POEMS SITTING IN THE DARK DURING A MAJOR POWER OUTAGE.
CRUSE
I'M YOUR NEPHEW HOWIE, AUNTIE MOO.
Type
Type
Type
Type
Type...
AND YOU NEVER KNOW WHEN THE LIGHTS MIGHT GO OUT AGAIN.
www.howardcruse.com

liliane in
Chicken-Head Love
©1999 Leanne Franson
So, here i was... my last year in art school, and a self-avowed dyke...
... with a wandering eye ...
well... NEVER did i say i was into women cuz i disliked guys...
Guillaume was quiet, tidy, discrete, and handsome in a pale, fragile way.
... and he wears an apron!!
That year we were the star ceramics pupils.
CERAMICS DEPT VALENTINES AUCTION
Hey! did you two see? Your sculptures got the highest auction bids! What talent!!
I was smitten with his nimble fingers, finely crafting a mythological avian universe.

And i became convinced he cared for me too.
...i can't go for dinner now cuz i'm going to the gym...
...we'll wait 'til you're done and all go together...
WOW!! He's WAITING for me!! He CARES!
So, i took it upon myself to reciprocate.
...can't get this bird's skull right... wish i had a model...
No, our chicken 'ave already no 'ead when we get dem... maybe Grand Boucherie near Jean Talon...
SAUCISSES
ROTI
BOUEF
POULET
What the heck! A 40-min. bike ride for LOVE...
Boy! Hope **they** have chicken heads!
It took alot of convincing that i was for real...
2

And a bit of pleading...
...please? ...it's for art...
It is illegal for 'ealth department... no give chicken 'ead!!
But finally they swayed!!
Oh, now he'd love me for sure!!
But then...
SSSSSSSSSSSSS...
They wouldn't accept my bike on the metro during rush hours...
KAFLUNPH..
KAFLUMPH KAFLUMPH..
damn...smells like dead chicken blood

The next day i dressed in my best straight-girl outfit.
?!
...for you!!
He did think it charming...
too weird!
...it's to use as a model, right? t'es fine!
But later, when i asked him to coffee...
...Sorry liliane, but i'm walking crystale 'ome
I drowned my woes in Purple Rain.
I only want to see you underneath the Purple Rain
Purple Rain
to see you
Purple Rain
I only want
crying
At that year's Christmas party:
You see, liliane, i was right... i knew you would be wit' a woman!
!?
And the chicken head?
merde! boiled it too long!
...gone all mushy!
4

-Sonnet 63-

Wm. Shakespeare + M. Fahy 1998

Against my love shall be
as I am now,
With Time's injurious hand
crushed and o'erworn;

When hours have
drained his blood
and filled his brow
With lines and wrinkles,

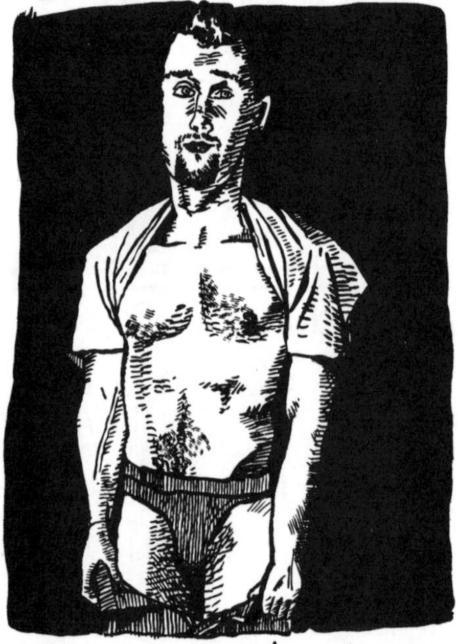

When his youthful morn
Hath traveled on to age's
steepy night,

And all those beauties
whereof now he's king
Are vanishing or
vanished out of sight,
Stealing away the treasure
of his spring—

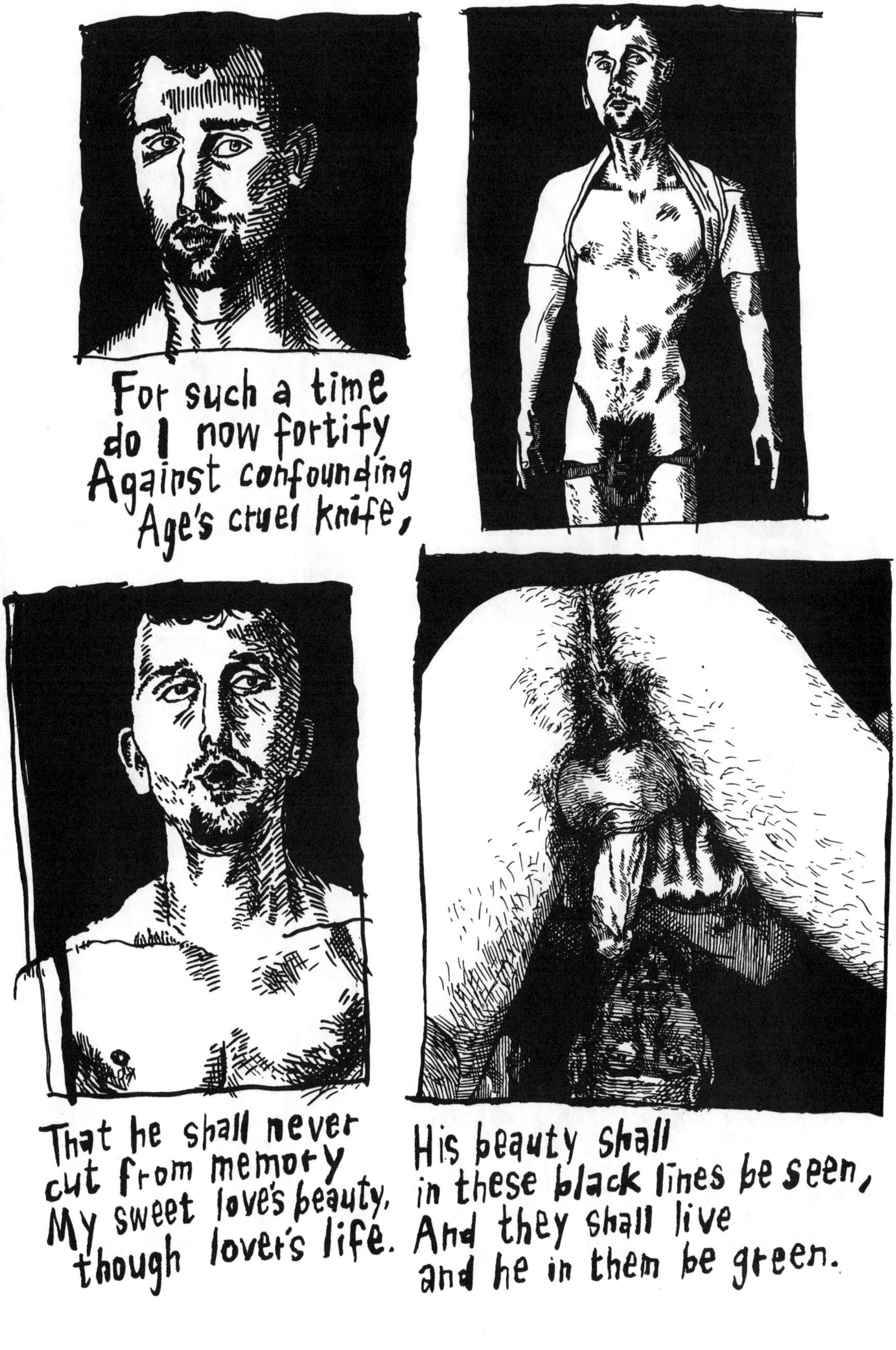
For such a time
do I now fortify
Against confounding
Age's cruel knife,
That he shall never
cut from memory
My sweet love's beauty,
though lover's life.
His beauty shall
in these black lines be seen,
And they shall live
and he in them be green.

CAMPER
©02
رمضان
RAMADAN
...eat and drink until the white thread of dawn appears to you distinct from its black thread. Then resume your fast until night falls.
al-Qur'an
al-Baqarah (The Cow), 187
HUH? SAMIRA?
SSHHH... GO BACK TO SLEEP. I'M GOING TO MAKE SUHOOR.*
I DON'T KNOW WHY YOU BOTHER...
SHHH... GO BACK TO SLEEP.
430 AM
* MEAL EATEN BEFORE DAWN
WHEN YOU THINK ABOUT BEING LEBANESE YOU THINK ABOUT LEMONS AND CONNECTING EYEBROWS.
IN YOUR MIND LEMONS ARE TRADITIONAL AND ARABIC.
PICK THE ONES WITH THIN SKINS, SAMIRA.
USE THEM AT ROOM TEMPERATURE AND YOU'LL GET MORE JUICE.
AND ALL YOUR RELATIVES HAD CONNECTING EYEBROWS. THE WOMEN WOULD SEPARATE THEIRS WITH SILVER TWEEZERS.
HOLD STILL! I'M TRYING TO MAKE YOU LOOK PRETTY!
AW, MOM! NOT NOW! I WANNA GO RIDE MY BIKE!
AHH... YOU'RE ONLY FASTING TO PROVE HOW TOUGH YOU ARE!
Mmm... MAYBE IT REMINDS ME WHO I AM.
I REMEMBER RAMADAN WHEN I WAS A KID. THERE WAS ALWAYS THAT FORTY POUND BAG OF DATES IN THE KITCHEN.
I FASTED EVERY YEAR FROM WHEN I WAS 13 UNTIL I WAS 19.
CHOMP
CHOMP
YOU DON'T MIND IF I EAT, DO YOU?

I WAS SUCH A SERIOUS KID. I WAS AFRAID TO BRUSH MY TEETH AFTER SUNRISE BECAUSE I MIGHT SWALLOW TOOTHPASTE.
I LOVED LISTENING TO THE QUR'AN, THE MONOTONY WAS SO RELAXING.
ONCE I THOUGHT I WOULD BE AN IMAM... STUDYING THE SHARI'A.*
A REAL 5 PILLARS GIRL.
*ISLAMIC LAW
I GOTTA GO. I GOT AN EARLY CALL TODAY.
KISS
REMEMBER- NO SEX UNTIL SUNDOWN!
I KNOW. AND THINK OF ALL THE LADIES WHO WILL BE DISAPPOINTED!
WAITING WILL ONLY MAKE YOU WANT ME MORE, HABIBTI!
YOU FIX COPY MACHINES. YOUR GIRLFRIEND WORRIES THAT YOU INHALE TOO MUCH TONER.
OH THANK GOD YOU'RE HERE!
BUT YOU LIKE YOUR JOB.
YOU'VE SAVED THE DAY!
THANKS SO MUCH!
HERE, HAVE A DONUT...
DONUTS
YOU USED TO LIE.
NO, THANKS, I'M ON A DIET.
OH, ME TOO! I JUST HATE HAVING THESE FIVE EXTRA POUNDS! DO YOU EVER THROW UP?
DONUTS
THEN YOU TOLD THE TRUTH.
NO, THANKS, I'M FASTING.
OH, ARE YOU A BUDDHIST?
NO, MUSLIM.
MUSLIM, RIGHT. THEY FACE EAST WHEN THEY PRAY.
NOT IN INDIA...
BUT ISN'T THAT THE RELIGION WHERE THE MEN BEAT THE WOMEN?
DONUTS

NOW YOU JUST REFUSE POLITELY. IT'S MUCH LESS COMPLICATED.
NO, THANKS. I JUST ATE.
DONUTS
I'M HERE TO FIX THE COPY MACHINE.
YOU?! THEY SENT A GIRL?
UH... I COULDA FIXED IT MYSELF, BUT I'M REALLY BUSY.
SURE...
PAPER JAM...
ALL FIXED! SIGN HERE.
HMMPH!
IN SOME WAYS GROWING UP ARAB PREPARED YOU FOR BEING A DYKE.
THE ENDLESS DISCUSSIONS ABOUT IDENTITY...
AN ARAB IS SOMEONE WHO SPEAKS ARABIC!
WHAT ABOUT IRAN AND ARMENIA?!
"MIDDLE EASTERN" IS TOO COLONIALIST!
"SOUTHWEST ASIAN/NORTH AFRICAN" IS MORE INCLUSIVE!
MORE CONFUSING!
SOME OF THOSE MARONITE CHRISTIANS THINK THEY'RE NOT ARAB!
NOT ALL ARABS ARE MUSLIM!
NOT ALL MUSLIMS ARE ARAB!
SUNNI?
SHI'A?
DRUZE?
SHE'S SUCH A DYKE!
YOU MEAN BUTCH?
SORTA BUTCHY FEMME!
A SOFT BUTCH?
I'D SAY HARD FEMME!
TOP? BOTTOM?
PRE-OP TRANS?
I HEARD SHE SWITCHES!
I THOUGHT SHE WAS BISEXUAL!
SHE SAYS SHE'S A LESBIAN WHO SLEEPS WITH MEN!
THAT'S BULLSHIT!
ARE WE DEFINED BY CULTURE OR SEXUALITY?

OUTING CELEBRITIES...
CASEY KASEM
JAMIE FARR
FRANK ZAPPA
TIFFANY
DICK DALE
DANNY THOMAS
KRISTY McNICHOL
KATHY NAJIMY
MARLO THOMAS
CALLIE KHOURI
PAULA ABDUL
DOUG FLUTIE
DR. DEBAKEY
JULIE TAYMOR
F. MURRAY ABRAHAM
PAUL ANKA
TINY TIM
TONY SHALHOUB
RALPH NADER
HELEN THOMAS
DONNA SHALALA
SELMA HAYEK
JODIE FOSTER
MELISSA ETHERIDGE
XENA + GABRIELLE
CHASTITY BONO
DUSTY SPRINGFIELD
QUEEN LATIFAH
WHITNEY HOUSTON
JOAN JETT
LIZ SMITH
SUSAN SONTAG
GERTRUDE + ALICE
ROSIE O'DONNELL
BARBARA JORDAN
k d lang
JANIS IAN
ELLEN DEGENERES
LILY TOMLIN
BILLIE JEAN KING
THE SEPARATION OF THE SEXES...
AND DON'T EVER LET A BOY TOUCH YOU OR LOOK AT YOU IN A BAD WAY!
YOU JUST STAY AWAY FROM BOYS!
OK.
IN CONCERT TONIGHT! WOMEN ONLY
GODDAM LESBIAN SEPARATISTS!
MAKING THAT SPLIT-SECOND DECISION ABOUT WHEN TO PUBLICLY IDENTIFY YOURSELF...
DID YOU SEE THOSE COOL PICTURES ON TV OF US BOMBING IRAQ?!
WE KICKED ARAB BUTT!
WELL...
CAN YOU BELIEVE THAT GAYS WANT TO ADOPT CHILDREN?
ISN'T THAT DISGUSTING?
WELL...
THE NEED TO KNOW SELF DEFENSE...
CAMEL JOCKEY! SAND NIGGER!
POW
DYKE! LEZZIE!
POW
BUT IN OTHER WAYS BEING ARAB-AMERICAN DIDN'T PREPARE YOU AT ALL FOR GAY LIFE IN THE UNITED STATES...
OH, SAMIRA, I'M GOING TO MARRY RAMZI - THAT GAY MAN I TOLD YOU ABOUT. IT WILL BE EASIER THIS WAY.
DON'T TELL ANYONE! IT REALLY IS A MATTER OF LIFE AND DEATH!
DYKE COUSIN VISITING FROM LEBANON.
ONLY OTHER QUEER ARAB YOU KNEW.

SURE, MY FAMILY TOLERATES ME AND MY GIRLFRIEND, BUT I WANT REAL RESPECT!
MY MOM HAD A FIT 'CUZ ME AND MY GIRLFRIEND WERE MAKING OUT ON HER FRONT LAWN! WHAT A PRUDE!
IF YOUR FAMILY DOESN'T ACCEPT YOU, JUST TELL 'EM TO GO TO HELL! YOU DON'T NEED 'EM!
?
SAMIRA IN COLLEGE
IX
ASSALAAMU ALAYKUM!
WA ALAYKUM AS SALAAM!
WHY AM I DOING THIS FAST?
RAMADAN IS A WHOLE MONTH!
WHAT AM I TRYING TO PROVE?
IS THIS SUPPOSED TO MAKE ME MORE SPIRITUAL? MORE MUSLIM?
FASTING IS SUPPOSED TO SHOW OBEDIANCE, NOT STRENGTH. BUT IT DOES MAKE ME FEEL TOUGH...
WHAT KIND OF MUSLIM AM I ANYWAY? I DON'T PRAY FIVE TIMES A DAY AND SOMETIMES I EAT BACON...
WILL FASTING MAKE ME APPRECIATE ALL THE COMFORTS I HAVE?..
...MAKE ME UNDERSTAND SUFFERING?
OR DO I JUST MISS MY FAMILY?
I'M SO HUNGRY...
WELL AT LEAST IT'S FALL...
...SUNSET COMES EARLY.

YOU THINK THE BEST THING ABOUT BEING PART OF AN ARAB FAMILY IS THE CLOSENESS.
SAMIRA! GIVE ME A HUG!
TASTE THIS!
MMM... MY FAVORITE!
YOUR COUSINS ARE UPSTAIRS.
AND THE WORST THING ABOUT IT IS THE CLOSENESS.
NO, YOU CAN'T STAY OUT THAT LATE!
YOU'LL SHAME THE FAMILY!
RESPECT YOUR FATHER!
WHEN YOU WENT AWAY TO SCHOOL YOU DID ALL THOSE THINGS YOU'D BEEN TOLD NOT TO.
SMOKING
SHORT HAIR
NO SCARF
GIRLFRIEND
NOT MUSLIM
ALCOHOL
NOT ARAB
SKIMPY CLOTHES
BUT YOU MISSED HAVING OTHER ARABS AROUND.
ISRAEL HAS A RIGHT TO BE IN LEBANON- IT'S SELF DEFENSE!
AND THOSE PALESTINIANS WANT TO TAKE OVER JERUSALEM!
TSK! THOSE ARABS ARE ALL A BUNCH OF TERRORISTS!
SOMETIMES IT WAS EASIER TO COME OUT AS QUEER THAN AS AN ARAB.
TERRORISTS?! I'LL SHOW YOU TERRORISTS! WACO, TEXAS- AMERICAN WHITE BOY! OKLAHOMA CITY- AMERICAN WHITE BOY! UNABOMBER- AMERICAN WHITE BOY! KILLERS OF ABORTION DOCTORS- AMERICAN WHITE BOYS! KILLINGS IN SCHOOLS- AMERICAN WHITE BOYS!
WHAT'S WITH HER?
SPUTTER! SPUTTER!
THEN YOU MET RANIA, THE EGYPTIAN IN YOUR HISTORY CLASS.
SECOND QUEER ARAB YOU KNEW.
SHE VEILED WHEN SHE WENT HOME. YOU LOVED KISSING HER IN THE HIJAB.
I'LL SEE YOU NEXT SEMESTER, HABIBTI!
I'LL MISS YOU, RANIA!
THE TWO OF YOU WRESTLED WITH CREATING A FEMINIST INTERPRETATION OF THE QUR'AN.
SURE IT SAYS A MAN CAN HAVE FOUR WIVES, BUT HE HAS TO TREAT THEM EQUALLY OR HE ONLY GETS ONE.
AND WHO COULD TREAT FOUR WOMEN THE SAME?
AND THERE'S NOTHING THERE ABOUT WEARING HIJAB OR CHADOR.
IT JUST SAYS TO DRESS IN A CONCEALING WAY.
"VEIL YOUR BOSOM." "DRAW THEIR VEILS CLOSE AROUND THEM."
BUT WHAT ABOUT ALL THAT "OBEDIENCE TO HUSBANDS" STUFF?

YOU SEARCHED FOR AN IDENTITY.
CHECK ONE:
CAUCASIAN
AFRICAN-AMERICAN
LATINO
ASIAN
OTHER
USUALLY YOU HAD TWO PICTURES TO CHOOSE FROM.
EVIL OR EXOTIC
YOU KNEW YOUR IDENTITY WAS RICHER THAN THAT. AND YET YOU ALSO SECRETLY GLORIED IN THE STEREOTYPES.
YES, BE AFRAID! BE VERY AFRAID!
TAKE ME!
YOU ARE A WALKING CONTRADICTION.
UNFEMININE WOMAN
ARAB BORN IN THE U.S.
LESBIAN WHO SPEAKS ARABIC
MUSLIM WHO EATS PUSSY
AND THEN YOU GO HOME FROM SCHOOL FOR WINTER VACATION.
WE KNOW ALL ABOUT YOU AND THAT GIRL!
YOU HAVE SHAMED THE FAMILY!
YOU'RE NO DAUGHTER OF MINE!
THERE ARE NO ARAB HOMOSEXUALS!
YOU'RE AN ABOMINATION!
WHAT DO I DO?
DO I HAVE TO CHOOSE BETWEEN MY FAMILY AND THE TRUTH?
COULD I LIVE A LIE? GET MARRIED? BE ACCEPTABLE?
COULD I GIVE UP MY FAMILY? MY CULTURE? THE FOOD? THE MUSIC?
SIGH
AARRGGHHH
SNATCH
SOB!

YOU VISIT YOUR FAMILY LESS OFTEN.
I MISS MY MOTHER'S SMELL...
BUT OVER THE YEARS YOU AND YOUR FAMILY CAME TO AN UNSPOKEN UNDERSTANDING. THEY TREAT YOU POLITELY, AND YOU KEEP YOUR SEXUALITY DISCREET.
HI MOM! THIS IS MY FRIEND ANNA!
WELCOME! SIT DOWN AND EAT!
NOW YOU'VE BEEN WITH YOUR GIRLFRIEND FOR SIX YEARS. THEY ACCEPT HER AS YOUR NICE ARAB ROOMMATE – EVEN THOUGH SHE **IS** CHRISTIAN.
HOW CAN SHE NOT KNOW?
DOES SHE REALLY THINK I DON'T KNOW?
AND THEN, SEPTEMBER 11 ARRIVED.
OMIGOD!
WHY DID IT HAVE TO BE ARABS? HOW COULD THEY DO IT IN THE NAME OF ISLAM? SOB
I DON'T KNOW, MOM...
DEPORTATIONS...
CALL FOR TRANSLATORS OF ARABIC + FARSI...
ISRAEL STEPS UP BOMBING
NOW THE U.S. HAS AN EXCUSE TO IGNORE ALL THE LEGITIMATE ARGUMENTS AGAINST IT'S FOREIGN POLICY!
IN TIMES OF CRISIS, YOU BOND WITH STRANGERS.
THEY ATTACKED NEW YORK! THEY ATTACKED WASHINGTON!
ARE YOU OK?
BOMB THE PALESTINIANS!
SUDDENLY, ARABS AND ISLAM WERE ALL OVER THE MEDIA.
IT TAKES A TRAGEDY LIKE THIS TO GET A U.S. PRESIDENT TO VISIT A MOSQUE?
THIS REMINDS ME OF HOW AIDS BROUGHT QUEERS INTO THE PUBLIC EYE.
PREZ TALKS TO ARABS
DOESN'T LISTEN
ARE ALL MUSLIMS EVIL?
GAS MASKS ON SALE
YOU BOUNCE BACK AND FORTH BETWEEN MOURNING...
MY COUSIN IN N.Y. WORKED IN THE WORLD TRADE CENTER. SHE DIDN'T MAKE IT OUT.
I'M SO SORRY...

...TO FEAR.
MOSQUE ATTACKED!
SIKH KILLED!
YOU GO ONLINE TO TALK TO OTHER ARABS...
America doesn't know what suffering is! This is NOTHING compared to Palestine or Bosnia or Viet Nam!
YEAH... THAT'S TRUE...
Who cares about a few dead Americans!
BUT THOSE WERE INNOCENT PEOPLE!
AT LEAST EVERYONE IS TALKING ABOUT GLOBAL POLITICS FOR A CHANGE...
BUT IS THIS GOING TO BRING PEOPLE TOGETHER OR CAUSE EVEN MORE DEATH?
I DON'T KNOW, HABIBTI...
THAT'S IT. I'M DONE FOR THE DAY...
SAMIRA! HOW'D IT GO TODAY?
CHOMPCHOMP I'M SO HUNGRY!
MILK
DATES
I SAW TWO WOMEN ON THE STREET IN HIJAB.
AND, YOU KNOW, I GOT SO EXCITED 'CUZ I KNEW THEY WERE FASTING, TOO!
AHH- FORCED VEILING IS RIDICULOUS!
STILL, IT'S A WAY TO CLAIM YOUR IDENTITY, ESPECIALLY IF YOU'RE IN THE MINORITY.
BUT IF ALL THE WOMEN WERE VEILED YOU'D BE EXCITED BY THE UNCOVERED WOMEN... THEY'D BE THE REBELS.
HMMM... I GUESS SO.
TSK! RELIGION WILL DRIVE YOU FUCKING CRAZY IF YOU THINK ABOUT IT TOO MUCH!
THANKS FOR YOUR ASTUTE THEOLOGICAL INSIGHT.

I MEAN LOOK AT YOU— A BIG OL' FASTING MUSLIM DYKE!
YEAH, I KNOW, IT SEEMS KINDA SILLY.
BUT... I DUNNO... IT'S FAMILIAR. IT'S COMFORTING. IT'S A WAY TO CONNECT WITH MY FAMILY, IT'S... CULTURE... IT'S HISTORY,... IT'S... IT'S...
DAMN! IT'S GREAT TO HAVE SOMETHING TO EAT!
SO... THE SUN'S DOWN... YOU KNOW WHAT THAT MEANS!
I'M GOING TO BED, HABIBTI...
KISS!
SAMIRA? YOU COMING TO BED?
CLICK!
THE QUR'AN
ARABIC-ENGLISH
FOR SHARING THEIR STORIES, I THANK:
AMAL
AMIRA
AISHAH
BASMA
DIALA
DALILA
FAZILET
HEBA
KHADIJA
LUBNA
MARIAM
NADYALEC
NAYLA
PARISA

YOU MUST NOT READ
GABRIEL GARCÍA MÁRQUEZ
AFTER THE BREAKUP
Joan Hilty ©2003
YOU MUST NOT READ GABRIEL GARCÍA MÁRQUEZ AFTER THE BREAKUP.
CAN'T SLEEP.
CAN'T EAT.
TIRED OF DRINKING.
PERHAPS IF I READ A LITTLE ...
3:51
One Hundred Years of Solitude
IT WILL ONLY MAKE MATTERS WORSE!
THE BOSSY SPIRIT MANIFESTATIONS WILL DAMPEN THE SYMPATHY OF YOUR FRIENDS.
WEAVE A MOURNING SCARF FROM BANANA LEAVES.
SO THEN SHE SLAMS THE DOOR, AN' :SNIF:
LOOK, I REALLY DO WANT TO LISTEN TO YOUR PROBLEMS BUT THIS APPARITION IS FREAKING ME OUT.
TIME WILL BECOME MEANINGLESS TO YOU.
HOW LONG ARE YOU GONNA BE IN THERE ALREADY ??!?!
LONG? WHAT IS "LONG"? IS IT ONE YEAR? FIVE? IF I WERE TO RUN OFF WITH THE GYPSIES, WHAT IS A DECADE? ¡NADA! IF I SET SAIL TO MACAU AND...
MURMURS
YOU REALIZE THIS MEANS SHE'S BATHING IN ACACIA BLOSSOMS AGAIN.
Another Crazy Guy Allowed To Own Gun
YOU WILL GROW ALL OBSESSED WITH INTERPRETING VISIONS.
WORMS!
I WAS MAKING SOUP AND IT'S BECOME WORMS! SHE WANTS ME BACK!
IT BECAME WORMS BECAUSE YOU PUT IT ON THE STOVE AND THEN LOCKED YOURSELF IN YOUR ROOM FOR TWO WEEKS.
WORST OF ALL, IT WILL SEVERELY IMPEDE YOUR CHANCES OF FINDING LOVE ANEW!
NITA! UM.. WAIT! PLEASE?
LOOK, EVERY TIME WE GO OUT, I GET ATTACKED BY SWARMS OF YELLOW BUTTERFLIES.
I'M JUST NOT THAT KIND OF GIRL.
SO DO NOT READ HIM.
YOU WILL ONLY REGRET IT.
I AM HAPPY READING PEOPLE MAGAZINE, I AM HAPPY READING PEOPLE MAGAZINE ......
People THE 50 UGLIEST PEOPLE
HOLY SHIT, THERE'S A BEDOUIN CARNIVAL AT THE FRONT DOOR.

JUNE 1999... BACK IN THE DAYS WHEN "GAY MARRIAGE" WAS STILL ONLY MAKE-BELIEVE...
VAN, DARLING— WE'VE COCOONED FOR NEARLY A YEAR AND... AND... AW, SHUCKS— VAN, WILL YOU MARRY ME?
OH MY GAAAWD!!
DEMETRIOS! MITZI! ALOYSIUS! WE'RE LEGITIMATE! HE PROPOSED!
OH, VAN, LET'S BE SO VERY HAPPY!
DON'T GET JEAWOUS, WUVVER!
YOU'LL ALWAYS BE THE PRIZE OF MY TEDDY BEAR COLLECTION!
Mitzi, Aloysius, and Demetrios cordially invite you to a
TEDDY BEARS' WEDDING
to celebrate the union of their loving daddies
Carlo Crapo
and
Van von Van
Romanesque Gardens, City Park
BYO
SO YOU'RE HAVING A WEDDING CEREMONY. I SUPPOSE YOU THINK YOU'LL NOW BE ABLE TO LIVE HAPPILY EVER AFTER!
WE JUST WANT TO SHARE OUR HAPPINESS WITH OUR LOVED ONES! AND WE WANT YOU TO BE OUR MATRON OF HONOR, SMARSHA!
"FAG-HAG OF HONOR" ...IT'S MORE HONEST!
IT'LL BE WONDERFUL! I SEE A CEREMONY ALL IN LAVENDER! AND BALLOONS EVERYWHERE!
I WOULD GUESS YOU'D DECIDE ON BLACK AND BLUE!
HA HA HA HA!
WELL, IF I MUST BE LABELED AND ACT OUT A ROLE...!
IT'LL BE IN THE ROMANESQUE GARDEN IN THE PARK—
THAT CRUISING GROUND...?
IT'S WHERE WE MET!
WE'RE WRITING OUR OWN VOWS!
OH YEAH? HOW ABOUT... "ANY EXCUSE FOR A PARTY!"
OR MAYBE... "YOU'LL DO UNTIL SOMEBODY BETTER COMES ALONG"
I CALLED THE PARKS DEPARTMENT AND ARRANGED EVERYTHING—! OF COURSE, I HAD TO TELL THEM THE BRIDE'S NAME IS "VANNA"!
BITCH!
OH, GO SHOPPING!

AND SO THEY DID!
PINK JACKETS WITH PEARL BUTTONS!
NO! LAVENDER WITH LACE!
LEATHER!
PUNK!
LIBERACE-WEAR!
ELTON JOHN!
HIP-HOP!
GOTH!
GROOM
KALVIN CLEIN
HOW COULD ONE CONSIDER ANYTHING BUT TRADITIONAL?!
HOW ABOUT NUDIST—? HEH HEH!
I KNOW! LET'S GO AS PAPER DOLLS!
SPARE US THE CORNY GIMMICKS!
IS THIS A WEDDING OR HALLOWEEN?

REHEARSAL DAY
IS EVERYTHING READY? I JUST KNOW SOMETHING IS GOING TO GO WRONG!
WHERE ARE THE BEST MEN?
HONEY, I'VE BEEN ASKING THAT QUESTION FOR YEARS!
NO, I MEAN—
WELL, DUH!
OH, HERE COMES VAN WITH SOMEONE NOW!
HI, EVERYONE! CARLO, THIS IS MICHAEL!
GREETINGS, CARLO! I EXPECTED ANOTHER BEAR! AND YET YOU'RE PERFECTLY HAIRLESS!
AND YOU'RE JUST AS FURRY AS VAN! BOY, HE SURE KNOWS HOW TO PICK 'EM!
OH, SO YOU'RE INTO HAIRY MEN?
UM, NO!
AREN'T ALL VAN'S FRIENDS?
HMM... HERE COMES STEVE, AT LAST!
VAN, THIS IS MY SCHOOL FRIEND STEVE!
STEVE, THIS IS VAN, MY FIANCE!
WELL, LOOK AT YOU! UH... I MEAN... NICE TO MEET YOU!
I'VE SEEN THIS SCENE IN FOUR OR FIVE DOZEN PORN MOVIES!
I'LL NEVER FORGET THAT TIME AT THE BATHS!
PLACES, EVERYBODY!
OKAY, WE START WITH THE BALLOON PAGEANT, POETRY RECITAL, TROTH-PLEDGING, AND SLOW-MOTION RUN INTO EACH OTHERS' ARMS!

AND THEN IT WAS "OUR WEDDING DAY"
I JUST KNOW THAT SOMETHING IS GOING TO GO TERRIBLY WRONG! WE'VE HAD TOO MANY CLICHÉS ALREADY, AND THE WEDDING IS JUST GETTING STARTED! WE'RE TEMPTING FATE!
WHERE ARE THE BEST MEN?
THERE AREN'T ANY.
HUH?
...AS PASTOR OF THE CHURCH OF CHRIST SAPPHO, IT IS MY DUTY TO JOIN TOGETHER CARLO AND VAN IN HOLY, IF UNOFFICIAL, WEDLOCK, BECAUSE IT'S BETTER THAN HAVING THEM MARRY WYMYN!
HA HA HA HA!
WE'LL NOW HAVE SONGS AND TABLEAUX TO CERTIFY THEIR DEEP RELATIONSHIP— POP! GODDESSDAMMIT!
POP!
OH GOD, THE WIND IS RUINING OUR GORGEOUS BALLOON BOUQUETS!
OH, I DON'T KNOW— I THINK IT'S KIND OF ROMANTIC!
"OH VANDY, YOU CAME AND YOU GAVE WITHOUT TAKING..."
POP!
POP!
OKAY, HERE WE GO! THIS IS WHERE CARLO AND I RUN INTO EACH OTHER'S ARMS IN SLOW-MOTION!
IT'LL BE JUST LIKE A SHAMPOO COMMERCIAL!
SPLA-WHAM!
HOW DO YOU RUN IN SLOW-MOTION, ANYWAY?

MEANWHILE...
LOOK, MOMMY, A WEDDING!
ISN'T THIS SWEET? HOW COLORFUL!
ZZZZ
OBVIOUSLY AN ATTORNEY
"I, CARLO, PARTY OF THE FIRST PART, TAKE THEE, VAN, PARTY OF THE SECOND PART, INTO..."
MOMMY, WHERE'S THE BRIDE?
ZZZZZ
"'WE WILL BUILD IT HERE,' SAID POOH, 'JUST BY THIS WOOD, OUT OF THE WIND, BECAUSE THIS IS WHERE I THOUGHT OF IT. AND WE WILL CALL THIS POOH CORNER.'"
WE PRONOUNCE YOU HUSBAND AND HUSBAND!
I WANNA SEE THE BRIDE!
COME ON, KIDS, LET'S GO!
ZZZZZ
WE'RE LEAVING RIGHT NOW!
NO NO NO! I WANNA SEE THE BRIDE!
CLAP CLAP CLAP
CLAP CLAP
MITZI! DEMETRIOS! ALOYSIUS! WE'RE MARRIED!!
I WANNA SEE THE BRIDE!

AT THE RECEPTION...
HMPH! I'LL BET MICHAEL IS TELLING CARLO ALL THOSE EMBARRASSING STORIES FROM OUR SCHOOL DAYS!
If you go down in the woods today,
SO, YOU SAY YOU'RE TOTALLY HAIRLESS—?
HMPH! STEVE IS TOO INTERESTED IN VAN'S BEAR FAMILY!
COOCHIE COO!
WHY, YOU FURRY THING!
you'd better not go alone...
ONE THING LEADS TO ANOTHER UNTIL...
I'M NOT LEAVIN' 'TIL I'VE SAT ON THE LAP OF EVERY MAN IN THE HOUSE!
AND I'M SICK TO DEATH OF THESE GODDAMN TEDDY BEARS!
MY BABIES!
POP!
...at six o'clock their Mummies and Daddies will take them home to bed...
Mitzi, Pooky, and Constance cordially invite you to a Lifelong Pledge between their loving daddies Steve Urino and Von van Von
Nondenominational Chapel, 4:00 p.m. Dickensian attire
SOME PEOPLE NEVER LEARN!
IF AT FIRST YOU DON'T SUCCEED, TRY AND TRY AGAIN, HUH?
Please join Carlo Crapo and Michael Manfest as we pledge our UNDYING LOVE
Clothing optional Riverside Park
2:30 p.m.
Because they're tired little Teddy Bears!
ONE LIFE TO LIVE
AND THAT'S HOW YOUR DADDY AND I GOT MARRIED!
©1999 ROBERT "I DESPISE CHEAP SENTIMENT" TRIPTOW
DEDICATED TO JUANITA, MY "MOTHER-OUT-LAW"
IT'S A DIFFERENT STORY WHEN A MARRIAGE IS RE
SEE "MATRIMONY, TEDDY BEAR STYLE" IN NAUGHTY BITS #

THE PARTY
©95
A CARTOON JAM BY:
(IN ORDER OF APPEARANCE)
1 JENNIFER CAMPER
2 Howard Cruse
3 DIANE DIMASSA
4 Rupert Kinnard
5 ALISON BECHDEL
6 Ivan Velez Jr.
HEY! WILL YOU HURRY UP IN THERE WITH YOUR PRIMPING?
BAM! BAM!
DAMN! I DIDN'T KNOW HAVING MY FAGGOT BROTHER FOR A ROOMMATE MEANT I WOULD NEVER GET TO USE THE MIRROR AGAIN!
BAM!
OH, CHILL OUT, ROXIE! EVERYBODY KNOWS THAT DYKES DON'T NEED MIRRORS!
ACNE GUNK
WHADDA YA THINK THEY PUT ALL THAT CHROME ON YOUR HARLEY FOR?
BOOM BOOM BOOM
WUTHA FUCK IZZAT!?
DISCO?
ALRIGHT, ALRIGHT, ALRIGHT, B.B.! I BET YOU WILL BE THE ONLY GAY AFRICAN AMERICAN SUPERHERO AT ROXIE AND ROB'S PARTY. I JUST HOPE THAT VILLAGE PEOPLE MUSIC I HEAR ISN'T COMING FROM THEIR PLACE!
BOOM BOOM BOOM BOOM
I SUSPECT WE'RE GOING TO ENCOUNTER SOMETHING EVEN STRANGER THAN 70s MUSIC AT THIS GATHERING!
UH... RIGHT NOW YOU TWO ARE ENCOUNTERING SHAMELESS CRUISING FROM THOSE WOMEN OVER THERE...
QUIT WHINING, MO! IT WON'T BE SO BAD. THAT COUPLA BABES LOOKS LIKE THEY'RE HEADED THIS WAY.
Y.M.C.A! BOOM BUDDA BOOM!
YEAH, AND SO DOES THE PSYCHO PUNK BEHIND 'EM, AND THE GUY WITH THE CAPE. HOW'D I LET YOU TALK ME INTO THIS? I HATE PARTIES!
ORGANIC WATER
WUTHA FUCK IZZAT!?
OOO.. I THINK I SMELL BIRKENSTOCKS!
EXCUSE ME, HON. SMALL ELEVATOR.
OH, THAT'S OK... REALLY... IT IS.
SHH. GOTTA REMIND ROXIE ABOUT THAT ARMS SHIPMENT COMING IN.
WHY DOES SHE ALWAYS GET CRUISED FIRST?
BE NICE.

ROB! TURN OFF THAT FUCKIN' DISCO AND PUT ON SOMETHING GOOD!
SIGH
THE SEVENTIES WERE THE BEST YEARS OF MY LIFE...
DING DONG
BOOM BUDDA BOOM
OH SHIT! THE GUESTS ARE HERE ALREADY!
I FEEL SORRY FOR THE YOUNG PEOPLE TODAY WHO'VE NEVER SAVORED THE PROFOUND SPIRITUAL RESONANCES OF DISCO... THE WAY IT TIES IN TO THE SENSUAL CAMPFIRE RITUALS OF THE PAGAN TRIBES OF PREHISTORY...
HI, EVERY-BODY.
...'SPECIALLY ON POPPERS!
In the Nay-vee!
GET THAT SHIT MUSIC OFF!
REALLY, ROX—DON'T YOU HAVE SOME MEG CHRISTIAN OR SOMETHING IN THE HOUSE?
ROXXXIIIEEE! NICE TO SEE YOU!
OOPS! 'SCUZE ME!
QUIT MESSIN' WITH THAT WHITE GIRL! SHE'S NERVOUS ENOUGH!
UM HMM
HEY! WATCH THE PERRIER!
OK, DISCO BALLS!! YOUR TIME HAS COME!
ENOUGH! SUCH VIOLENCE MUST NOT BE TOLERATED! DRASTIC STEPS MUST BE TAKEN! ONLY B.B. AND I HAVE THE POWER TO TRANSPORT THIS PARTY TO OUR NATION'S CAPITOL!
WHY DON'T YOU TWO GO ON AHEAD? GOD, SUPER-HEROES ARE SUCH A DRAG AT PARTIES. ALWAYS TRANS-PORTING THINGS.
YOUR TITS... THEY'RE SO... WELL-DRAWN!
YO, ROB! LONG TIME NO SEE! YOU SHOULD COME DOWN TO TH' GYM MORE OFTEN!
DISCO INFERNO!
GNNR!
BY GOLLY, I BET YOU'D LIKE SOME NICE RAP MUSIC! WHAT SAY LET'S GIVE MY VANILLA ICE ALBUM A LISTEN?!
THAT'S THE SPIRIT! LET'S FUCK!
I WANT MY MOMMY.
HI! WE'RE BACK!
OH MY.
HUH? IN FRONT OF EVERYBODY?
JEEZ, ROXY! DOES IT ALWAYS GOTTA BE ONE OF THOSE PARTIES?
WAIT! LET GO! OH GOD! T..T.. THAT'S NOT PC!
ORGY!
C'MON, MO! I'VE GOT A 12 INCH DILDO WITH YOUR NAME ON IT!!
LOOKS LIKE WE GOT BACK JUST IN TIME!
HOT DAMN!
SQUEEZE
TSK TSK
GEE ROB—I DIDN'T KNOW YOU COULD WRESTLE!
F.T.W.
SHIT, I YANKED TH' FUCKER'S HEAD OFF!
PUH-LEEZ! I NEVER DO ROUGH SEX AT MIXED PARTIES!
ROXIE! YOUR BROTHER'S A CYBORG??
I KNEW THERE WAS SOMETHING DIFFERENT ABOUT HIM FROM AN EARLY AGE!
HEY RATSY, CMERE! I NEED YA TO HOLD ROXXIE DOWN!
OH, ALLOW ME!
THESE LESBIANS ARE CRAZY!
Y-YEAH!

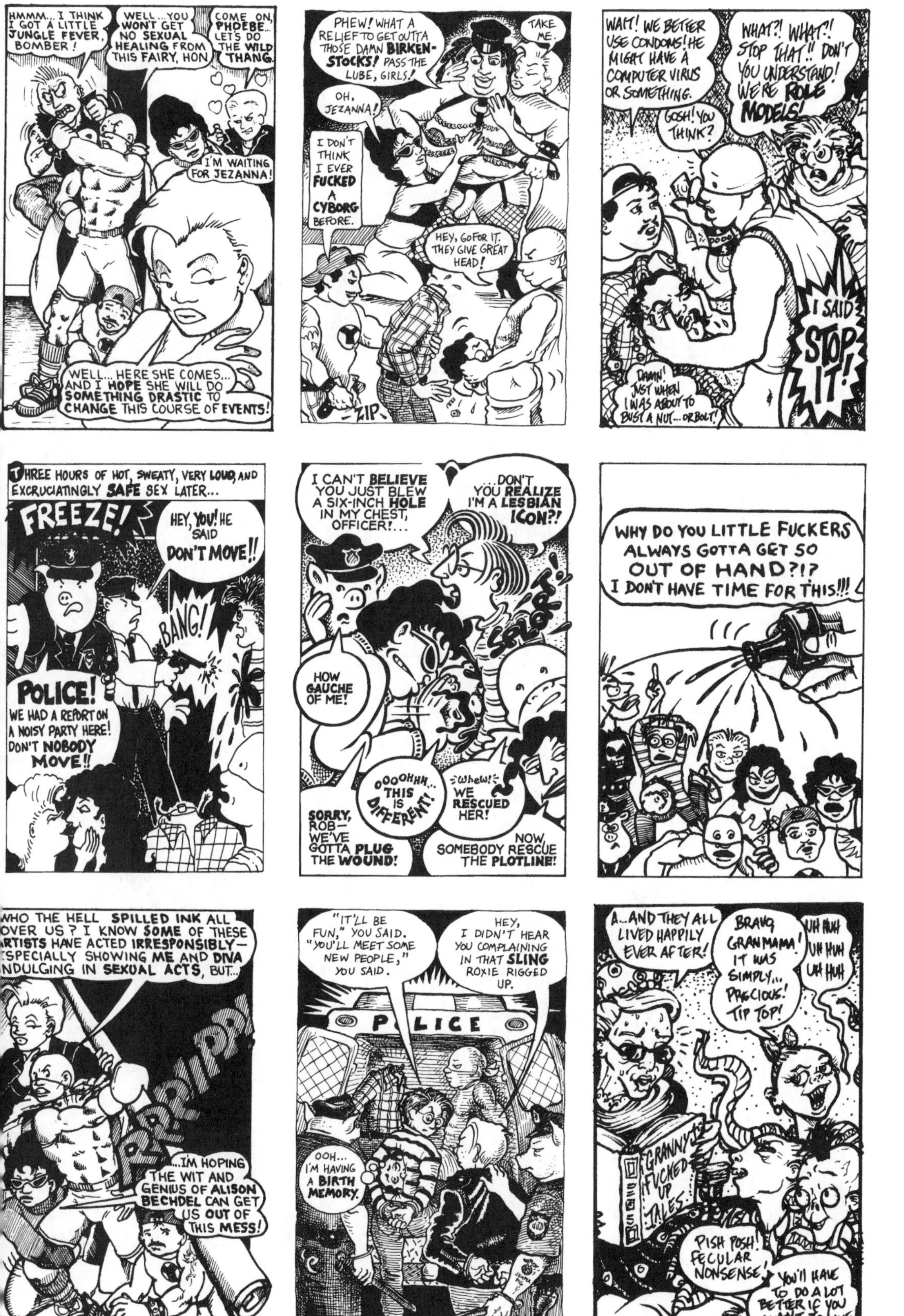

HMMM... I THINK I GOT A LITTLE JUNGLE FEVER, BOMBER!
WELL... YOU WON'T GET NO SEXUAL HEALING FROM THIS FAIRY, HON
COME ON, PHOEBE... LET'S DO THE WILD THANG.
I'M WAITING FOR JEZANNA!
WELL... HERE SHE COMES... AND I HOPE SHE WILL DO SOMETHING DRASTIC TO CHANGE THIS COURSE OF EVENTS!
PHEW! WHAT A RELIEF TO GET OUTTA THOSE DAMN BIRKEN-STOCKS! PASS THE LUBE, GIRLS!
TAKE ME.
OH, JEZANNA!
I DON'T THINK I EVER FUCKED A CYBORG BEFORE.
HEY, GO FOR IT. THEY GIVE GREAT HEAD!
ZIP
WAIT! WE BETTER USE CONDOMS! HE MIGHT HAVE A COMPUTER VIRUS OR SOMETHING.
GOSH! YOU THINK?
WHAT?! WHAT?! STOP THAT!! DON'T YOU UNDERSTAND! WE'RE ROLE MODELS!
I SAID STOP IT!
DAMN! JUST WHEN I WAS ABOUT TO BUST A NUT... OR BOLT!
THREE HOURS OF HOT, SWEATY, VERY LOUD, AND EXCRUCIATINGLY SAFE SEX LATER...
FREEZE!
HEY, YOU! HE SAID DON'T MOVE!!
BANG!
POLICE! WE HAD A REPORT ON A NOISY PARTY HERE! DON'T NOBODY MOVE!!
I CAN'T BELIEVE YOU JUST BLEW A SIX-INCH HOLE IN MY CHEST, OFFICER!...
...DON'T YOU REALIZE I'M A LESBIAN ICON?!
SPLORT!
HOW GAUCHE OF ME!
OOOOHHH... THIS IS DIFFERENT!
Whew! WE RESCUED HER!
SORRY, ROB— WE'VE GOTTA PLUG THE WOUND!
NOW, SOMEBODY RESCUE THE PLOTLINE!
WHY DO YOU LITTLE FUCKERS ALWAYS GOTTA GET SO OUT OF HAND?!? I DON'T HAVE TIME FOR THIS!!!
WHO THE HELL SPILLED INK ALL OVER US? I KNOW SOME OF THESE ARTISTS HAVE ACTED IRRESPONSIBLY— ESPECIALLY SHOWING ME AND DIVA INDULGING IN SEXUAL ACTS, BUT...
RRRIIPP!
...I'M HOPING THE WIT AND GENIUS OF ALISON BECHDEL CAN GET US OUT OF THIS MESS!
"IT'LL BE FUN," YOU SAID. "YOU'LL MEET SOME NEW PEOPLE," YOU SAID.
HEY, I DIDN'T HEAR YOU COMPLAINING IN THAT SLING ROXIE RIGGED UP.
POLICE
OOH... I'M HAVING A BIRTH MEMORY.
A... AND THEY ALL LIVED HAPPILY EVER AFTER!
BRAVO GRANMAMA! IT WAS SIMPLY... PRECIOUS! TIP TOP!
UH HUH UH HUH UH HUH
GRANNY'S FUCKED UP TALES
PISH POSH! FECULAR NONSENSE!
YOU'LL HAVE TO DO A LOT BETTER IF YOU WANT TO LIVE.

Ariel schrag Feb. 13 2002
home for the holidays.
Beean
byan.
red T-shirt's in the house.
Anne isn't.
Hubbard's done gone crazy.
oh you!
mom!
showdown.
showdown?
and Shmoby, from time to time.
who's there!
Toby and Ariel!
There was the skin doctor
ACNE
so what's this about?
I have some moles.
the breast doctor.
so what's going on?
I have some lumps
the Dalai Lama
and the physical therapist.
good.
tomorrow is the throat doctor.
I'm sorry to say, but you have both tuberculosis and cystic fibrosis.
Meli on the phone.
Mellie's place!
Joshua suzanne got breast implants!
raspy polyps!
Mellie's place.
I go by byan.
and danger in my dreams.

MY NAME IS LARITZA FULANO, AND I DON'T LIKE TO EAT SHIT.
BUT THERE I WAS, MUNCHING IT LIKE IT WAS CHEETOS.
COMPLIMENTS OF THE BLESSED SISTER SANGANA PENDEJA DE LA ESTUPIDA AND HER SELF RIGHTEOUS BLAH BLAH BLAH
IT WAS ENOUGH TO DRIVE ANYBODY KOOKOO FOR COCOA PUFFS.
OKAY. I GET THE POINT!
CUT THE SHIT ALREADY!
WHAT?
YOU AIN'T DEAF! YOU HEARD WHAT I SAID. I DON'T HAVE MY BOOK REPORT!
BIG FUCKING DEAL!
IF YOU WANNA KILL ME FOR IT, THEN GO AND GET A GUN! OTHERWISE--
--JUST SHUT THE FUCK UP.
SHIT.
KRAK
KRAK
KRAK
SO I GOT SENT TO SEE MR. WERT, WHO REALLY HAS IT IN FOR ME JUST 'CAUSE I PUT A LITTLE SUGAR IN HIS GAS TANK A COUPLE OF TIMES BUT NEVER GOT OFFICIALLY CAUGHT. I HAD TO THINK FAST.
OF COURSE, IT DIDN'T HELP THAT HIS SECRETARY HATED MY GUTS.
FAITH IS FUN
YOU AGAIN. Tch Tch Tch.
BITCH.
SITTING NEXT TO ME WAS MISSY PISSY BAGGY EYES, WHO PROBABLY GOT SENT DOWN FOR SLEEPING IN CLASS AGAIN. SHE WAS ALWAYS DOING THAT SHIT.
AND SHE NEVER HAD TWO WORDS TO SAY TO ANY-ONE.
IN A WAY, YOU HAD TO RESPECT THAT.

BUT, OF COURSE, JUST AS I WAS THINKING THAT MAYBE MISSY PISSY WASN'T SO BAD AFTER ALL...
--THAT BOOGER COMES CRAWLING OUT HER NOSE.
SO I TURNED MY BACK ON HER.
?
HMPH.
MISSY PISSY BAGGY SAGGY BOOGER WOOGER. YUCK.
BESIDES. I HAD TO PREPARE FOR MY PERFORMANCE
ALRIGHT, YOUNG LADY. I'M READY FOR YOU NOW.
KEEP THE EYES BIG AND WATERY. MAKE HIM THINK YOU'RE SCARED.
SO... YOU REALLY THINK YOU CAN SPEW FILTH AT A DEDICATED TEACHER AND WALK AWAY CLEAN?
NO, LITTLE GIRL. YOU HAVE GONE TOO FAR THIS TIME.
SIT STILL. SHAKE THE HANDS LIKE YOU'RE NERVOUS.
OKAY. KNEES TOGETHER. WATER YOUR EYES A LITTLE. DROOL A LITTLE...
I'M CALLING YOUR GRANDMOTHER. THERE MIGHT EVEN BE SUSPENSION INVOLVED.
NOW GO FOR THE KILL.
I KNOW. I KNOW. I'VE BEEN SO TERRIBLE IT'S JUST...
MY FIRST PERIOD CAME TODAY... OUTA NOWHERE...
AND... AND... I JUST--
--SNAPPED!
OH GOD WHY DID I DO IT WHY?! SISTER TERESA IS A SAINT! A SAINT! SHE ONLY WANTS TO HELP ME LEARN!
HOW COULD I DO THIS TO HER!
HOW?! OH GOD! WHY!?
OH!
OH!
OH!
I THINK I JUST GOT A CRAMP.

A QUICK TRIP TO THE NURSE'S OFFICE AND THAT WAS THAT.
I EVEN GOT TO SKIP HISTORY AND TAKE A NAP.
I WAS THE TEEN QUEEN AND I KNEW IT.
AND SHE--
--WAS MY TOTAL OPPOSITE.
HAH! MISSY PISSY BAGGY EYES!
GOT YOUR PAMPERS ON TODAY?
HAW HAW HAW
I SMELL SOMETHING FUNNY AND IT'S NOT THE LUNCH!
HEY!
AIEEK!
SPLOOT!
HEY! WHAT THE HELL ARE Y--
YOU.. UH... OH-OKAY.
THIS SCHOOL IS FULL OF STUPID ASSHOLE JERKS.
STUPID ASSHOLE JERKS THAT KNOW NOT TO FUCK WITH ME.
WELL, MOST OF THEM KNOW.
AW, JEEZ.

SO MISSY PISSY SAT DOWN NEXT TO ME.
AND I LET HER.
AND SHE'S BEEN LIKE MY PUPPY DOG EVER SINCE.
LUCKY ME.
SHE EVEN FOUND OUT I LIVE, LIKE, DOWN HER BLOCK.
I WAS DOOMED TO BE BORED.
AND DESTINED TO HAVE MY GOOD NAME SOILED LIKE HER UNDERWEAR.
BUT THAT'S NOT THE POINT! OKAY, MAYBE IT IS. JUST A LITTLE.
I MEAN, LOOK AT HER! SHE'S A MESS!
HER HAIR'S STRINGY! SHE HAS NO STYLE WHATSOEVER.
AND TO TELL THE TRUTH SHE DOES SMELL A LITTLE TANGY.
SO HOW COME I STARTED NOT TO MIND SO MUCH?
WHY DID I GET SO PROTECTIVE OF HER?
MAYBE BECAUSE, UNDERNEATH THOSE BAGS AND THAT SPLOTCHY SKIN AND THAT MIASMA...
I COULD SMELL A SECRET.
AND NOT SOMETHING TACKY OR DEPRESSING AND AWFUL LIKE BEING MOLESTED OR HAVING TWELVE TOES--
--BUT SOMETHING DAMN JUICY AND AMAZING.
AND, HONEY, THAT WAS A SECRET I HAD TO KNOW.
AND WISH I NEVER FOUND OUT.

OKAY, SO WE FAST FORWARD AHEAD ABOUT TWO MONTHS.
DON'T COMPLAIN. I ONLY GOT NINE PAGES TO TELL THIS THING AND THAT WAS ONE MORE THAN I'M SUPPOSED TO.
MISSY PISSY, OR RATHER MELISSA, WAS STILL ACTING LIKE MY SHADOW. SHE'S EVEN GOT US MATCHING FRIENDSHIP BRACELETS.
CHEESY OR WHAT?
AND I WAS GETTING A LITTLE BORED WITH IT ALL.
WANNA GET SOME ICE CREAM AFTER SCHOOL?
NO.
HOW ABOUT SOME BURGERS?
NO.
HOW ABOUT SOME PIZZA?
NO.
AND YOU KNOW WHAT HAPPENS TO NERDY LONERS WHO FINALLY FIND A SUCKER WHO'LL TOLERATE THEM?
THEY DON'T EVER SHUT THE FUCK UP!
SHE WAS PARTICULARLY CHATTY TODAY BECAUSE IT WAS HER BIRTHDAY AND I PROMISED TO STAY AT HER HOUSE FOR A SLUMBER PARTY.
JUST ME AND HER.
OH JOY.
AND I KNOW THE IDIOTS WERE TALKING ABOUT US.. SAYING WE WERE CO-MUNCHING
AS IF. IN THEIR DREAMS.
SHIT. IF I WAS GONNA GO MUFFY, IT WOULD BE FOR SOMEONE MORE FABULOUS THAN MISSY PISSY BAGGY EYES.
WANNA GO TO THE COMIC BOOK STORE?
NO.
WANNA PLAY VIDEOS?
NO.
BUT WHAT IF SHE DID TRY SOMETHING TONIGHT?
WANNA GO SEE SOME OLD XENA SHOWS?
OH MY GAWD I GOTTA GET OUTA THIS!
UNFORTUNATELY MY ALCOHOLIC GRANDMA HAD OTHER PLANS.
WHATCHOO LOOKIN AT? DON' GIMME DAT LOOK!
BUT 'BUELA. I GOT CRAMPS!
SO WHAT? CRAMPS ARE GOOD FOR JOO. MEANS JOO A WOOMAN!
PLANS THAT INCLUDED ME BEING OUT OF THE HOUSE SO SHE COULD GET GOD KNOWS WHAT FROM GOD KNOWS WHO.
YUCK.

BUT, 'BUELA! I FEEL SIC--
OKAY. OKAY. GOO' NIGHT! HAVE A GOO' TIME!
SHE COULDN'T WAIT FOR ME TO GET OUT!
BRRR!
DOUBLE BRRR!
DRATS. FOILED AGAIN.
MISSY'S FAMILY WAS AS SAD AND CREEPY AND BAGGY-EYED AS SHE WAS...
...BUT THEY WERE ALSO JUST AS NICE, IN THAT ANNOYING NEEDY KIND OF WAY.
AND AS SAD LITTLE MISSY BLEW THE CANDLES--
--ON HER SAD LITTLE CAKE, I COULDN'T HELP BUT SMILE--
--AND HOPE HER SECRET WISH COMES TRUE.
CORNY, HUH?
AND HEY, IF SHE WANTED, SHE COULDA TOUCHED MY TITTY. AFTER ALL, IT WAS HER BIRTHDAY.
BUT NO FINGERPOPS!
BUT SHE DIDN'T. WE WERE ASLEEP BEFORE 'CHEERS'.
I DIDN'T EVEN FEEL WHEN HER FOLKS PUT US TO BED.
I WAS SLEEPING SOUNDLY
WELL, AS SOUNDLY AS I COULD IN A STRANGE HOUSE
WHICH WASN'T SOUND ENOUGH

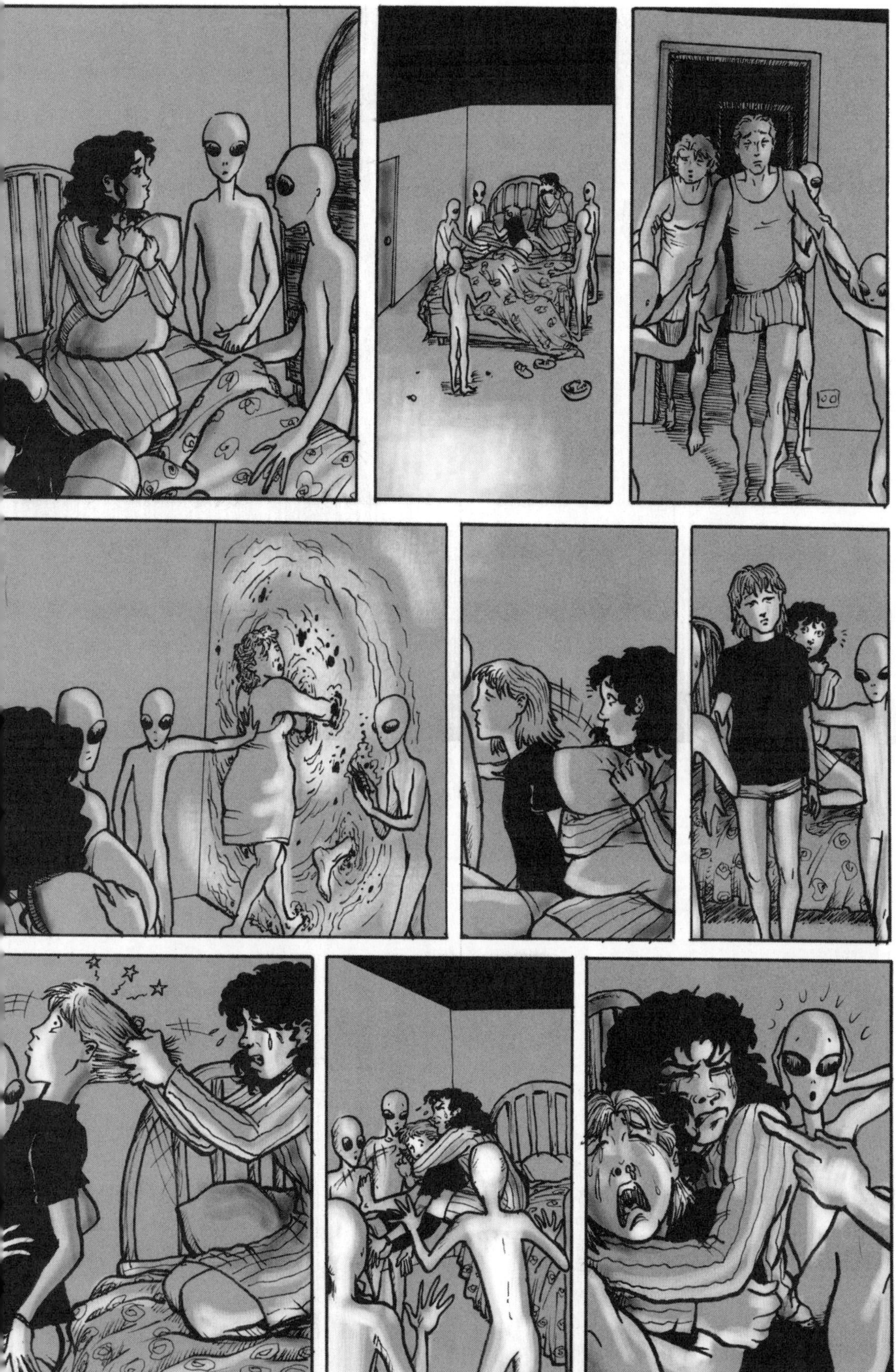

WE NEVER TALKED ABOUT WHAT HAPPENED. AFTER A WHILE IT ALL SEEMED LIKE A BAD DREAM.
BLAH BLAH BLAH
A BAD DREAM WE ALL HAD AT THE SAME TIME
MISSY AND HER PARENTS MOVED AWAY ABOUT A MONTH LATER. I DON'T BLAME THEM.
AT LEAST I FOUND OUT WHY MISSY HAD THOSE BAGS UNDER HER EYES.
AS FOR ME, I'M FINE.
I'M ALWAYS FINE
IT TAKES MORE THAN BUGHEADS TO MAKE ME FEEL LIKE SHIT.
BESIDES... THEY NEVER BOTHERED ME AGAIN. GUESS THEY DIDN'T HAVE TIME TO TAG ME.
EXIT
POOR MISSY.
I STILL THINK ABOUT HER AND HOPE SHE'S OKAY
EVEN THOUGH SHE PROBABLY ISN'T.
SHE WAS A HUGE PAIN IN THE ASS BUT KINDA COOL TOO.
FROM WHAT I HEAR, ONCE THE CREEPS TAG YOU, YOU'RE TAGGED FOR LIFE.
BUT THEN AGAIN, WHO ISN'T.
CHEESE POOFS
MISSY AND HER FOLKS GOT TAGGED AND THERE'S PROBABLY NOTHING THEY CAN DO ABOUT IT.
BUT AT LEAST I KNOW, IN SOME SMALL WAY...
...I TAGGED ONE OF THEM BACK.
LARITZA VERSUS THE SPACE ALIENS
by Ivan Velez Jr. 11/97

R MEMBER
GUY-PAUL
MORIN
REMEMB
GEORGE
JACKSON
ATTICA!

Look! Look! Look! Look!

This is a special day.
This is the day Delta gets out of jail
Delta is so happy.

Here is Peanut.
She is Delta's best friend.
She is taking Delta out to celebrate.

Pictures G.B. Jones Story Jennifer Camper

See Delta and Peanut celebrate! They are having a good time.
How many bottles can they drink?

LOOK! LOOK! Dancing Girls! The Dancing Girls are pretty!
See Delta smile. Hear Peanut laugh.
The Dancing Girls are fun!

Oh! Oh! Some people are being rude to the Dancing Girls! Now Delta and Peanut will teach them a lesson. See Delta kick ass! Hear Peanut crack heads!

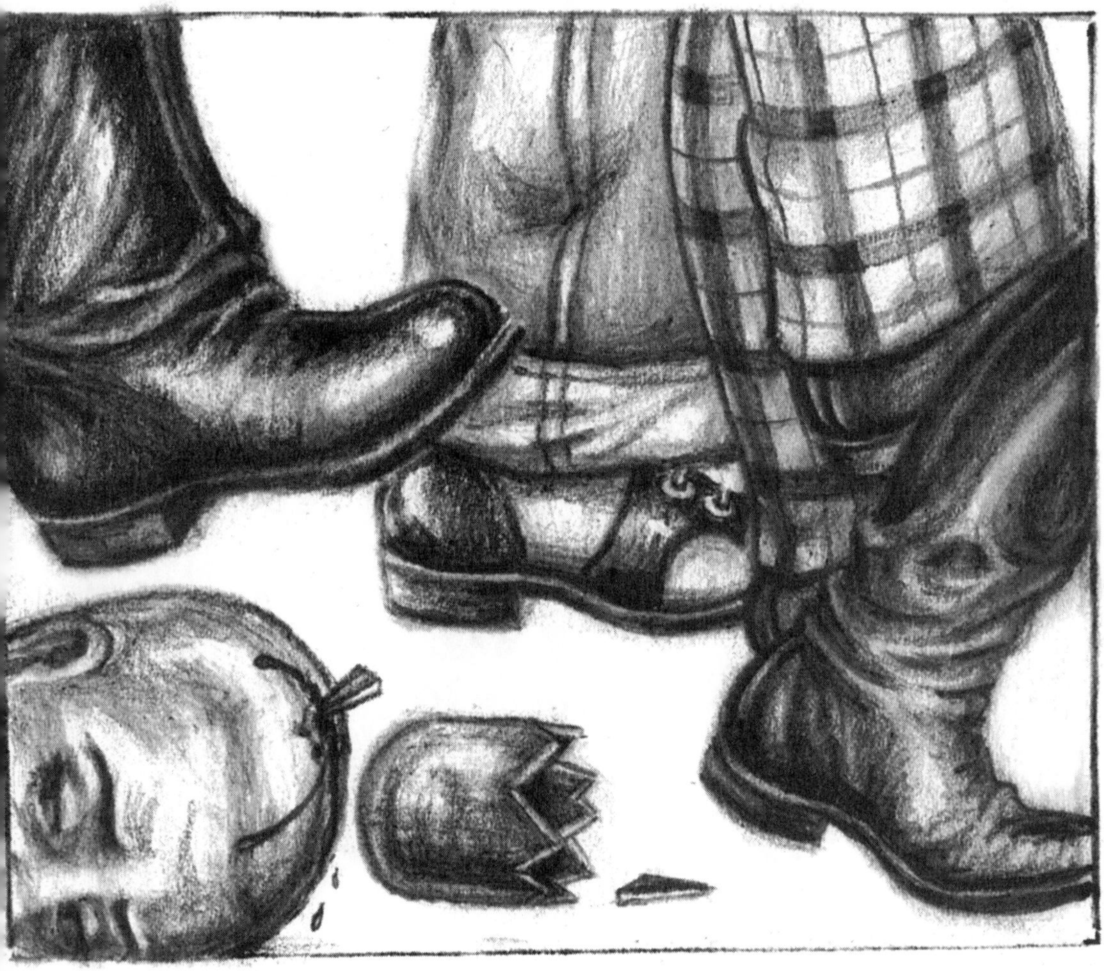

Run! Run!

Here come the cops!
Delta runs fast.
Peanut runs fast.
Will the cops catch them?

LOOK! LOOK! Delta and Peanut are safe at home. Who is with them? Two Dancing Girls! Now they will all celebrate some more. "Welcome home Delta", says Peanut. "You're the best Peanut," says Delta. "It is good to have a friend."

The End

contributors

Alison Bechdel's comic strip *Dykes to Watch Out For* has become a cultural institution for lesbians and discerning non-lesbians all over the planet since it first appeared in 1983. The strip runs in over 60 LGBT, feminist, and alternative publications in North America and the UK. Bechdel's tenth collection, *Dykes and Sundry Other Carbon-Based Life-Forms To Watch Out For,* has just been published by Alyson Books. Check out her website at www.dykestowatchoutfor.com.

Oppressed Minority Cartoonist: I was asked to contribute a piece to the Seattle alternative weekly paper *The Stranger's* annual queer pride issue in 2002. The theme was, "what I know now..." The editor wanted material about stuff you might have wanted to know, or could have been helped by knowing, but which you only found out through your own miserable experience. I appreciated the chance to vent.

The Party (group jam): I liked having the opportunity to sully my politically correct reputation a bit.

Media: The art is your basic india ink on Bristol, belabored endlessly in Photoshop because I was learning how to use my new Wacom tablet.

Jennifer Camper is a cartoonist and graphic artist whose work can be found in comic books, magazines, newspapers, anthologies, museum exhibitions and on various bathroom walls. Her books include *Rude Girls and Dangerous Women*, a cartoon collection, and *subGURLZ,* a graphic novel about three twisted women living in abandoned subway tunnels.

Ramadan: I wanted to write about friends of mine, Arab and Iranian dykes coming to terms with Islam. I'm Lebanese-American, but not Muslim, so I was nervous about truthfully documenting someone else's experience. I interviewed a group of women and wrote this fictional story based on their words. I wrote it in the second person as if I was telling their story back to them. The comic was written in 2000, but after the events of September 11, 2001, I went back and added those events to the story.

The Party (group jam): I love doing jams. It's very intimate and kinda sexy to draw each other's characters and to give up control.

Media: Penciled on smooth 2-ply bristol, then inked with brush. Lettered with technical pen. Reverses, tweaking and obsessive corrections in Photoshop.

Howard Cruse was the founding editor in 1980 of *Gay Comix* and the creator of *Wendel,* a comic strip that was regularly featured through most of the 1980s in *The Advocate*. In 2001 the entire *Wendel* series was collected in book form by Olmstead Press under the title *Wendel All Together*. Among Howard's other books was the award-winning graphic novel *Stuck Rubber Baby,* which since its 1995 publication by Paradox Press has been published overseas in German, Italian, French, and Spanish translations. Howard's newest book, an illustrated fable created in collaboration with Jeanne E. Shaffer and called *Th Swimmer With a Rope In His Teeth,* was published 2004 by Prometheus Books. Readers may sample wide spectrum of Howard's comics and cartoon effo by visiting his web site, Howard Cruse Centr (www.howardcruse.com).

Auntie Moo's Typewriters is dedicated to the mem ry of my mom, Irma Russell Cruse, who died in 200 The comic strip was drawn several years before h death, while her Alzheimer's was still in the process coaxing her into darkness.

Media: India Ink on 2-ply Bristol, burnished digita with Photoshop.

Diane DiMassa, the missing creator of *Hothe Paisan,* has decided It's Time again. The website is launched (www.hotheadpaisan.com) and a Hothe musical (that's right, musical) is in the works in collab ration with Animal (of Bitch & Animal.) It will be po tially showcased at the infamous Michigan Womer Festival this year, where I swore I would never go. I fe the one thing I CAN do in the face of this conservati take-over is assert my freakish and disgusting existen as much as possible. So I plan to crank out as mu crapola and propaganda as possible from now on.

Must Be Love was San Francisco inspired, if it's n obvious, and I took my time with it. People who are outside the mainstream having the same problems everyone else (duh). Everyone is carrying somethin So be nice. I drew it for something that never got pu lished and was listening to a lot of the Pixies a Massive Attack at the time.

The Party (group jam): I loved doing this jam w these girls & boys because they are all lunatics. It's li playing tag-team Top This psycho cartoon thru the mc The story always ends up so far out there, and I ca believe how sick everyone is. It makes me feel so vc dated. If I ever get caught and committed, I hope th are all there with me. What did I listen to while I dre Who the hell can remember, but probably Patti Sm and the Pixies.

Media: I like to char the end of my nose with a B lighter, file it to a point, and draw with it on regular o Bristol Board.

Michael Fahy Mr. Fahy is from Philadelphi "Philadelphia – We're History!"

Sonnet 63: This was inspired by Lynda Barry's *the All* from 1991. I thought that a meeting Shakespeare and *Honcho* was long overdue.

Leanne Franson is a bi-dyke living in Montreal, di ping her toes into the edge of middle age. She has ve little time for cartooning now since her night job of ch dren's illustrator keeps her chained to the drawi table and her mind out of the gutter. Look for her ch dren's books in bookstores and online. Since 1991 s has done 32 *Liliane* self-published minicomics, and h two books out called *Assume Nothing: Evolution of*

-Dyke and *Teaching Through Trauma*. You may order er books or reach her at inkspots@videotron.ca

Chicken-Head Love: This is a true story about the aditionally feminine wiles I use to seduce men I like. It oesn't work.

Media: Technical pen on tracing paper.

oan Hilty is the creator of the comic strip *Bitter Girl,* istributed by Q Syndicate, which follows the romantic dventures of a bunch of big-city dykes and runs week- at PlanetOut.com. Her work has appeared in the *illage Voice*, the *Advocate*, and *Girljock Magazine,* mong others. By day, she works for The Man as an ditor at DC Comics.

You Must Not Read Gabriel García Márquez after e Breakup: I really did try to get over a breakup by eading *One Hundred Years of Solitude*. What was I inking? This was rejected as a *Bitter Girl* script by an ditor who didn't think readers would know who arcía Márquez was, then added apologetically, "But en again, I'm not up on my lesbian novelists."

Media: Bristol board, technical pens, and Photoshop

. B. Jones also appears in *Boy Trouble,* edited by obert Kirby and David Kelly, *This Is The Salivation rmy,* edited by Scott Treleaven, and on the cover of *ugar Needle,* edited by Corinna Fastwolf. Past work an be found in *Dangerous Drawings,* edited by ndrea Juno.

Look! Look!: Any occasion that allows for the undermin-g of the values of our present society is a welcome one!

Media: A pencil and a piece of paper.

rof. I.B. Gittendowne aka **Rupert Kinnard** orn in Chicago IL., and after earning a degree in art Cornell College in 1979, Rupert Kinnard has been onored with various design awards through The Rupe roup Graphics for such organizations as The lational Organization for Women (N.O.W.), Gay unshine Press and many other organizations. In 1996 e was honored with the Portland's Spirit of Pride ward for community service. Among his published orks, *B.B. and the Diva: a collection of Cathartic omics featuring The Brown Bomber and Diva Touché ambé* was published in 1992. Original comics have lso been included as part of the San Francisco artoon Museum's permanent collection. The Brown omber and Diva Touché Flambé were also included the theatrical production of *Out of the Inkwell* at San rancisco's famed Theater Rhinoceros, in 1994. He onsiders his most awe-inspiring accomplishment to be s 13 year relationship with the world's greatest part-er, Scott Stapley.

The Party (group jam): This experience was the most n I've ever had that didn't involve bodily fluids. I did d the way some of the other artists treated the per-ona of the ever-so-dignified Diva Touché Flambé a bit candalous. Mostly I was just in awe to be included in jam that featured all of the other queer artists that I've dmired for so long.

Media: Duo-tone board and fine pointed felt tip arkers.

Robert Kirby has been drawing the self-syndicated comic strip, *Curbside* since 1991. The most recent paperback collection is *Curbside Boys* (Cleis Press). He is also the founder and co-editor of the gay boy comics anthology *Boy Trouble,* the latest edition of which was published in the spring of 2004 by DK Press (ordering info: David@davidkellystudio.com). Robert lives in Minneapolis. Email: curbside2@earthlink.net

Dollface (writer): I did it because Jen told me to, and because I wanted to work with Stephen Winter, a singularly fabulous human being.

Media: India ink on smooth 2-ply Bristol board

Serena Pillai aka **Serpilla** Born in November 1960, Scorpio. I'm a teacher in a state school in Cagliari, Sardinia (Italy). Very interested in art, I'm a supporter of the oppressed and the exploited, animals included. I passionately love women as you can see in my comic, *The Amazon Nightmare,* my second work, which is available on the Internet (www.ellexelle.it). The only problem is it is in Italian! Enthusiasts as well as horrified readers can mail their comments at sserpilla@supereva.it

The Italian Cousin: This work was originally intended as a gift to all women, and that's why it was first published on the Internet as free download material. Special thanks for the translation in English to Sally Davies.

Media: ink on paper

Karen Platt is an artist who has lived and worked in NYC since 1996. Her paintings and drawings have been exhibited nationally and internationally. She studied cartooning with Charles Burns in the early 80s at Washington University in St. Louis and later worked as an assistant to Peter Gross on *The Books of Magic, Ghost Rider, The Mask,* and other projects. Karen did several cartoons for the *Big Book* series in DC's Paradox line and has also been published in *Deadline Magazine*. Her cover art and illustrations have been featured in a variety of books and publications. Platt is currently working full-time in the advertising industry in New York, as well as continuing to freelance as an illustrator, storyboard artist, and cartoonist.

Front and Back Covers: Jen wanted a rowdy group of ladies whooping it up for the Celebration theme so I drew on my firsthand extensive "research" of the NYC lesbian club scene. I hope I've captured some of the flavor.

Media: I penciled and inked the cover by hand, later cleaning up lines and doing the color work in Photoshop.

Ariel Schrag is the author of the autobiographical comics books *Awkward, Definition, Potential* and *Likewise,* which chronicle her four years at Berkeley High school. Other side projects of Ariel's include: *Sinful Cynthia* (a choose-your-own-adventure-porn), *Linen and Things* (a collection of assorted comics drawn between 1997 and 2003) and *Rhymin' with no Hymen* (a collection of characters reciting whimsical rhymes.) Ariel's current projects include writing the screen adaptation of her third book, *Potential,* for Killer

Films; continuing work on *Likewise,* which is being published in an eight-issue series; and putting together a collection of short stories about her college years. *Awkward, Definition, Potential* and *Likewise* can be ordered from SLG publishing at www.slavelabor.com or 1-800-866-8929. Ariel can be contacted at arielschrag@hotmail.com

Wandering Hands: The night before I graduated from college my best friend Melissa spent the night with me in my dorm bed. Inspired and amused by the idea of two lover's tentative first touches Melissa's hand wandered over to me in the bed. I immediately shrieked and convulsed in horror, and then returned the favor. Wandering Hands.

Home for the Holidays: During my spring semester of junior year of college I studied abroad in Berlin. The school semester times are different in Germany than they are in America, so instead of having the usual two-week-holiday-break between semesters, I spent an elongated three months living at my mom's house in Oakland before leaving for Germany.

Media: Ink on paper

Robert Triptow The details of my life won't fit into one paragraph, and you really don't want to know anyway. Trust me. Whaddaya mean I have to tell 'em something... All right already. My quest was to become the Last Underground Cartoonist of the Haight/Ashbury, where I lived for a big chunk of my life and was published in classix like *Bizarre Sex* and *Young Lust*. Oh, yeah, I also edited *Gay Comix* for a while ("the funny ones"). *Real Girl, Strip AIDS U.S.A., Naughty Bits, Filth, Holy Titclamps,* and now *Juicy Mother*... (Why do the folks back in Yewtah think I do sex comix?) Lately I've been spending time again with my comix muse. I'm not sure if that's a good thing. My comix muse is a mean whore who usually will go home with anyone but me. Some of the fruits of our unholy union can be seen at www.roberttriptow.com.

Teddy Bears' Wedding was a failed project for the late '80s anthology, *Real Girl,* long before gay marriage was a news story. Events were lifted from a hilariously disastrous ceremony in Golden Gate Park. (I drew some frames from photos. After I'd finished the art, I realized I'd subconsciously recreated the old *Sugar & Spike* paper dolls, complete with drooling baby mouths. Now we know what little Spike grew up to be. *Teddy Bears' Wedding* was almost pulled from Juicy Mother because attitudes shifted due to the same-sex marital events of early 2004. I feared that readers would no longer understand that I was mocking self-indulgence and artifice. They'd probably think I was slamming same-sex marriage itself. My solution was to modify the original story a little and to draw a sequel with a happier ending. I urge anyone who enjoyed *Teddy Bears' Wedding* to look up *Matrimony, Teddy Bear Style* in *Naughty Bits #40*.

Media: Written and laid out on the computer, then penciled onto print-outs. Inked onto Bristol over a lightbox. Slathered with white-out to correct mistakes. *Teddy Bears' Wedding* was my last cartoon inked wi a yellow Koh-i-noor artpen (no longer manufacture that produced everything I've ever published. Mc Groening has the last one in the world. I want it.

Raised in the South Bronx, **Ivan Velez. Jr.** wa heavily influenced by the chop-socky karate flick *Astro Boy* cartoons, blaxploitation films, Spanish soa operas, and Silver Age comic books that filled eve second of his free time. So far, that hasn't changed. H work has also been seen in several issues of Ga *Comics, Details* magazine, *NYQ*, and *HX*. He has sol scripts to HBO and the Hudlin Brothers. He has als been reviewed in the *Advocate, Edge,* the *Villag Voice,* NPR, and the *New York Times*. Ivan has writte several Milestone titles, especially *Blood Syndica* (which included character design for some of the cas *A Man Called Holocaust,* and a year-long run on th acclaimed series *Static*. Both *Blood Syndicate* an *Static* have won awards on his shift.

Ivan has also written for the mainstream, bless his tle soul. He scripted the last two years on *Ghost Ride Abominations*, and a *Venom* mini-series, among othe for Marvel. At DC Comics, he wrote the *Eradicat* mini-series, did some hard time on *Extreme Justice*, an a story for Vertigo's *Flinch*. He continues to do the od *Power Puff Girls* story at their kid division.

But Ivan is mostly known as the creator of *Tales the Closet*, a ten-chapter graphic novel that depicts th lives of eight gay teenagers in Queens. Things loo very favorable for the completion of the last issue an the beginning of a new sequel, especially since most the ownership issues have been ironed out.

Laritza Versus the Space Invaders: Well, just lik everyone else, my life was threatened if I didn't hav the strip done in two weeks. That was, uh, six years ag

Media: HB, F, 2H pencils, Vellum finish Brist Board, any available cheap black marker (guarantee to fade in a year), and a kneaded rubber eraser. Als Photoshop is lovely as a cleaning tool, and sure mad my blacks blacker and whites whiter.

Stephen Winter is a writer, filmmaker, producer an visionary instigator. He's directed films like *Chocola Babies* and *Private Shows,* written scripts for Madonn Queen Latifah and Macy Gray, shilled for Lifetim VH1, the BBC and *The Ricki Lake Show,* won lots awards and accepted them gladly. He is very proud be the producer of *Tarnation* by Jonathan Caouett which had its 2004 world premiere at the Sundanc Film Festival and was accepted to the Cannes Fil Festival (Director's Fortnight).

Dollface (writer): This story has been adapted in about three screenplays of mine but always got cut f some damn reason. Many dear thanks to Jen and Kirk for affording me the opportunity to finally get this out my system as my first entree into the fabulous comi book-making club. What was my process in writin *Dollface?* Rolled some kale, grooved to Ranc Crawford, closed my eyes and thought of Franc Loving it! Living it! Needing much more...

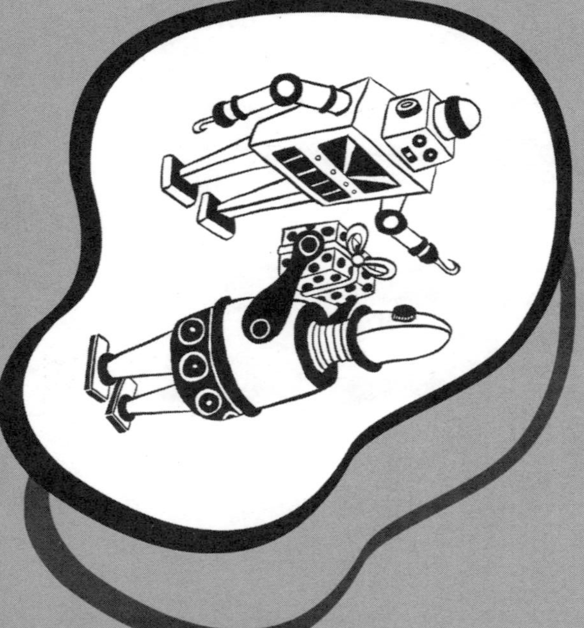